TEXAS
CELEBRITY
COOKBOOK

Russell M. Gardner
Chris Farkas

Library of Congress Catalog Number 84-082018
International Standard Book Number 0-9613874-0-8

Additional copies may be obtained by addressing:

Texas Celebrity Cookbook
Gardner-Farkas Press, Inc.
P.O. Box 33229
Fort Worth, Texas 76162

TEXAS CELEBRITY COOKBOOK may be obtained for
fundraising projects or retail outlets at wholesale rates.
Write above address for more information.

LIMITED EDITION 2,500

FIRST EDITION, NOVEMBER 1984, 10,000

SECOND EDITION, DECEMBER 1984, 10,000

THIRD EDITION, MAY 1985, 10,000

FOURTH EDITION, NOVEMBER 1985, 15,000

FIFTH EDITION, MAY 1986, 30,000

PRINTED BY WIMMER BROTHERS, INC.
5930 LBJ FREEWAY
DALLAS, TEXAS 75240

FOREWORD

Texas Celebrity Cookbook has been created specifically for the Texas Sesquicentennial Celebration. Over sixteen months in the making, more than 300 recipes were gathered from loyal Texans who wanted to participate in the event. The personality and interest of the individual is reflected in every recipe from Alan Bean's "Spacey Spaghetti Sauce" to the King Ranch's recipe, "Dinner For Two From The Wild." The fact that this book was created by Russell M. Gardner, a university student shows an exciting aspect of the celebration in that citizens of all ages may participate. This shows a dynamic quality in young Texans.

The founders of the Republic of Texas consumed a vastly different diet than we are accustomed to today. Similarly, when the Texas Bicentennial year of 2036 approaches, our descendants will delight in looking back upon our present day eating habits and preferences.

As for now, it is our desire that you enjoy using your Texas Celebrity Cookbook!

—*F. Chris Farkas*

ACKNOWLEDGMENTS

Russell M. Gardner
Special Thanks To:

Lady Bird Johnson
Mrs. Jane Justin
  *Compiler and publisher of "Mother Jane's
  Prescription for Hunger"*

Dr. Nell B. Robinson, Ph.D, RD, LD
  *Professor and Director of the Coordinated
  Undergraduate Program in Dietetics
  Texas Christian University
  Fort Worth, Texas*

Dr. Ben H. Procter, Ph.D
  *BA, University of Texas at Austin
  MA, University of Texas at Austin
  Ph.D, Harvard University
  Professor of History
  Texas Christian University
  Fort Worth, Texas*

Nan Mulvaney
Hart Graphics, Inc.

Cover Design and Graphics
  Louis Daniel

Back Cover Art
  Jack Bryant

Foreword
  F. Chris Farkas

Division Page Commentary
  David Clinkscale

Photography
  Texas Highways Magazine
  Dr. William R. Gardner
  Fort Worth Chamber of Commerce
  Lee Angle

Thanks To:
Jack Rattikin, Jr., Judy Alter, William E. Evetts, Richard
E. Miles, C. Harold Brown, Teresa Cage, Norma Crow,
Fran Chiles, Hub Baker, John Ratliff, Vivie Rowan, Bill
Wofford, Charles Mayberry, H. E. Dickey, Jr., Charles
A. Ringler, Buckshot Price

INTRODUCTION

In 1986 Texans throughout the world are revering, through celebrations, their sesquicentennial—and for good reason. In 1836 the actions and accomplishments of their forefathers had far-reaching effects on both Texas and the United States. At the Alamo late in February, William Barrett Travis, James Bowie, Davy Crockett, Jim Bonham, Almeron Dickinson, and a small force of 178 men valiantly fought a Mexican army (of at least 2,500 soldiers) under Antonio Lopez de Santa Anna. After thirteen days of courageous defense, during which at almost anytime the Texans could have escaped, they were overrun; however, they left a glorious heritage for all freedom-loving people. In the words of Travis, whose ideas reflected the feelings of the men at the Alamo, they would "fight with desperation, and that high souled courage which characterizes the patriot, who is willing to die in defence of his country's liberty and his own honor." And then he concluded by announcing: "God and Texas—Victory or Death."

While the men at the Alamo were suffering their final days on earth, a determined group of forty men (eventually increasing to fifty-nine), at Washington-on-the-Brazos were speaking to generations of Texans and Americans with equal resolve. Led by Sam Houston and Lorenzo de Zavala, they chose Richard Ellis of Red River as chairman who, in turn, appointed a committee, headed by George C. Childress of Milam, to write a declaration of independence. On March 2, 1836, they presented a document which was thereupon adopted and which was much like the American declaration of July 4, 1776. For example, the committee substituted the word "Mexico" for "Great Britain" as well as stating that it was the duty of government "to protect . . . lives, liberty, and property." And when a government failed to accomplish those ends, the people had "a sacred obligation . . . to abolish such government and create another in its stead." Two days later, March 4, in order to provide a defense for Texas, they selected Sam Houston as commander of all armed forces; they ordered Texas commissioners to the United States—Stephen F. Austin, William H. Wharton, and Branch T. Archer to borrow $1,000,000; and they proceeded to write a new constitution for Texas. On March 16, after almost two weeks of continual work, they adopted a document which was easy to understand and strong enough to work. Besides providing for an executive branch of government which called for a president and vice-president to be elected for three-year terms (but who could not succeed themselves), they established a bicameral congress—made up of a senate and house of representatives—a system of federal courts which would effectively maintain the checks and balances theory embodied in the United States Constitution, and a declaration of rights which was similar to the American Bill of Rights. Then at 4 a.m. on March 17 they elected David G. Burnet as president and Lorenzo de Zavala as vice-president of the Republic of Texas, their term of office extending until September 1, 1836, when Texans would vote upon acceptance of their new constitution and would elect their first permanent public officials.

But to safeguard these actions and to preserve such freedoms, Sam Houston had to provide for the common defense of all Texans—and that goal would not be easy. By March 11 he had reached Gonzales enroute to San Antonio with an assortment of 374 men which in no way resembled an army. But on the night of March 13, Mrs. Dickinson and several wives and children of the defenders of the Alamo arrived with news of what had happened—Bowie, Travis, Crockett, and their men had all been killed, their bodies ingloriously burned in a common funeral pyre. The result was like a fire bell in the night. Houston ordered an immediate retreat, known in Texas History as the "Runaway Scrape." The Texans initiated a scorched-earth policy. Whether soldiers or civilians, what they could not carry they destroyed or burned and then began retreating eastward from Santa Anna's advancing army.

For five weeks this discouraging experience continued; the Texans stopped briefly for short rests on the Colorado River near La Grange and at the Brazos River. Within this time their plight became even more discouraging as news of Mexican victories over Texan forces at San Patricio and Refugio reached them. Then to their grief and horror they learned that late in March, 1836, Santa Anna had ordered the bloody execution of Colonel James W. Fannin and his army of approximately 400 men who had surrendered near Goliad. Now they realized what fate was in store for all rebels; therefore, both their terror and anger increased. Near Buffalo Bayou on April 20, however, Sam Houston allowed Santa Anna to "trap" him. Selecting an excellent position to defend against attack, Houston at first prepared against a Mexican frontal assault which would cost the enemy dearly. But by the next day, after a short conference with his officers, Houston decided to gamble everything. At half past three in the afternoon, while the Mexican army which was tired from the ordeal of marching across Texas, was taking a siesta, he ordered his men to advance. Taking the enemy by surprise, the Texans routed the Mexican army after eighteen minutes—many fleeing soldiers were now unarmed and tried to surrender, yelling "Me No Alamo—Me No Goliad." Not until sundown, after their anger had been spent, did they begin to take prisoners as

★ I N T R O D U C T I O N ★

Houston and several of his officers had earlier commanded. Yet the Texan victory was not complete until the next day when a squad of men captured Santa Anna. Upon being escorted to a large oak tree where Houston lay painfully wounded, his ankle smashed by a bullet, the Mexican commander announced with great dignity and pride: "I am General Antonio Lopez de Santa Anna, and a prisoner-of-war at your disposition." And then, as if to explain the importance of the Battle of San Jacinto, he added: "You have conquered the Napoleon of the West."

For such heroic deeds, for such outstanding valor, Texans are paying homage to those men and women who helped carve a new republic and then a state out of a wilderness, who created institutions of lasting value for their descendants, and who established freedom and liberty in this turbulent land.

Ben H. Procter
Texas Christian University

DEDICATED TO

DR. AND MRS. WILLIAM R. GARDNER
COL. AND MRS. FRANK FARKAS
MR. AND MRS. THEODORE PIBIL
MR. AND MRS. STEARNS H. GARDNER

IN MEMORY OF

MR. AND MRS. E. P. MADDOX, JR.

"Hot off the presses . . . the TEXAS CELEBRITY COOKBOOK, which has all of the ingredients for becoming an international best seller."
—*ULTRA MAGAZINE*

"While Michener bangs out his novel of Texas, that will surely be turned into a television movie, Russell M. Gardner, a student at Texas Christian University, and Chris Farkas, the owner of the Mama's Pizza chain, have turned out what has to be the Texas cookbook to end all Texas cookbooks."
—*DENTON RECORD-CHRONICLE*

"The book delights the reader with its wealth of favorite recipes from celebrities from all walks of life."
—*AMARILLO DAILY NEWS*

"From Don Meredith's recipe for making pimiento cheese to Dan Rather's brisket of beef to Barbara Bush's decadent chocolate mousse, the book is spiced with historic bits of lore and photo's of Texana as well as down right interesting recipes."
—*THE HOUSTON POST*

"Unlike many cookbooks, this one has a personality which becomes evident upon casually glancing through it."
—*SALADO VILLAGE VOICE*

"Russell M. Gardner has come up with one of the best-selling state-sanctioned Texas Sesquicentennial projects to hit the state."
—*TEMPLE DAILY TELEGRAM*

"There is as much emphasis on personality as there is on food. For example, a couple of the recipes are Alan Bean's Spacey Spaghetti sauce and the King Ranch recipe for Dinner for Two from the Wild."
—*CISSY, THE FORT WORTH STAR-TELEGRAM*

"Gardner's final collection of famous Texas personality recipes is impressive: author Larry L. King, heiress and real estate developer Caroline Hunt Schoellkopf, Barbara Bush . . . TCU coach Jim Wacker, Kenny Rogers, Carol Burnett, and a host of Texas mayors, United States Senators, politicians, and even a recipe from president Reagan."
—*THE DALLAS MORNING NEWS*

"The Texas Celebrity Cookbook, created for the 1986 Texas Sesquicentennial, features more than 300 recipes from Texas politicians, athletes, news casters, movie stars, and other prominent figures."
—*TEXAS HIGHWAYS MAGAZINE*

CONTENTS

Surrender of Santa Anna
at
San Jacinto Battlefield April 21, 1836

Surrender of Santa Anna
at
San Jacinto Battlefield April 21, 1836

Exact copy of painting by Huddle which hangs in the lobby of the
Texas State Capitol
Copied by Margaret Brisbine

Presented to
The Fort Worth Club
by
Amon G. Carter

Reproduction authorized by Senate resolution

LAJ Ranch

Stonewall, Texas

Mrs. Lyndon B. Johnson's recipe for

Cheese Wafers

1 cup margarine or soft butter
2 cups flour
8 oz. sharp cheddar cheese, grated
1 teaspoon cayenne pepper
1/2 teaspoon salt
2 cups puffed cereal (rice crispies)

Cut butter into flour; add cheese and seasonings; fold in
cereal. Drop by small rounds on ungreased cookie sheet
and flatten with spoon. Bake at 350 degrees for about
15 minutes. (don't get too brown !)

RUTA'S OWN

An excellent little appetizer.

Put consommé gel into individual serving dish or glass.
Pour one jigger of vodka over gel. Spoon sour cream over
gel and vodka. Garnish with caviar and tops of green onions
chopped.

CITY OF SEGUIN

HOT ARTICHOKE SPREAD

1 (14 oz.) Can artichoke hearts, drained, and chopped
1 Cup mayonnaise
1 Cup grated Parmesan Cheese
1/2 Teaspoon garlic power

Combine all ingredients, mixing well.
Spoon into lightly greased three (3) cup casserole.
Bake at 350° for 20 minutes.
Serve with assorted cracker.

Yield: 2 1/2 Cups.

Betty Jean Jones
Mayor

CANAPE MARGUERY

One of the best recipes from one of the finest old New York restaurants.

1 (7-ounce) can water-packed tuna,
    drained and flaked
12 anchovy fillets, chopped
¾ cup chopped green pepper
½ cup chopped pimento
1 egg, hard-cooked and chopped

1 cup Russian dressing
1½ tablespoons cognac
6 tablespoons butter
6 thin white bread slices, crusts
    removed
1 tablespoon Worcestershire sauce

In medium bowl, combine tuna, anchovies, green pepper, pimento, egg and 2 tablespoons Russian dressing. Mix well and set aside. In small bowl, mix remaining Russian dressing with cognac and set aside. In hot butter in a chafing dish or larger pan, sauté bread until well browned and butter absorbed. In same pan, spread tuna mixture over bread. Cover with Russian dressing mixture. Sprinkle ½ teaspoon Worcestershire sauce over each. Heat over low heat for 5 to 10 minutes or until very hot. Serve immediately.

Electra Waggoner Biggs
W. T. Waggoner Estate

CRAB DIP SUPREME

Party favorite.

1 (6 to 7 ounce) can crab, drained
1 cup mayonnaise
½ cup sour cream
1 teaspoon chopped parsley

1 tablespoon sherry
1 teaspoon lemon juice
Salt, to taste
Pepper, to taste

Pick crab to remove shell fragments. Mix with remaining ingredients. Chill at least 2 hours before serving. Makes 2 cups.

Mrs. R. P. Klein (Mary Beth)
Wife, Mayor of Amarillo, Texas

CRAB MOUSSE

1 small package cream cheese
1 can cream of mushroom soup
8 ounces crab meat
1 cup mayonnaise
1 small onion, finely chopped
1 cup finely chopped celery

1 package Knox unflavored gelatin
3 tablespoons cold water
Pimento, to garnish
Olive slices, to garnish
Parsley, to garnish

Heat and blend cream cheese and mushroom soup. Mix well with crab meat, mayonnaise, onion and celery. Dissolve gelatin in water, and blend into crab mixture. Pour into a wet fish mold and chill overnight. Decorate the fish with pimento, olive slices and parsley. Serve with sesame seed crackers.

Lynda Johnson Robb
First Lady of Virginia

GATE OF SPAIN DIP

2 cups mayonnaise
1 or more tablespoons curry powder
1 teaspoon lemon juice
1 teaspoon Worcestershire sauce

1 teaspoon A.1. steak sauce
1 teaspoon black pepper
½ teaspoon celery salt
Dash Tabasco sauce

Mix all ingredients. This is an excellent dip for buffet use. Serve with carrot sticks, celery, cucumber, radish, turnip, cauliflower, squash, etc.

Mrs. William P. Hobby, Jr. (Diana)
Wife, Lt. Governor

TONY SLAUGHTER DIP

1 pint Hellmann's mayonnaise
1 envelope Lipton's onion soup mix
1 (8-ounce) carton sour cream
Juice of lemon half

1 (8-ounce) bottle horseradish
Dash salt
Cooked shrimp bits (optional)

Mix all ingredients. Chill. For extra flavor, add the shrimp bits. Don't dip with potato chips–they break too easy. Use corn chips.

Tony Slaughter
Columnist
Fort Worth Star-Telegram

LAKE CHARLES DIP

1½ pints sour cream
3 tablespoons mayonnaise
1 package Good Seasons Italian
  Dressing mix

1 teaspoon Tabasco sauce
Juice of ½ lemon
4 avocados, diced
1 tomato, diced

Combine all ingredients and use with fresh vegetables.

Mrs. Stuart Schuster

HERB CURRY DIP

1 cup mayonnaise
½ cup sour cream
1 teaspoon crushed mixed herbs (Fines
  Herbes by Spice Island)
¼ teaspoon salt
2 teaspoons capers

⅛ teaspoon curry powder
1 tablespoon parsley flakes
1 tablespoon grated onion
1½ teaspoons lemon juice
½ teaspoon Worcestershire sauce

Blend all ingredients and chill.

Mrs. Al Worn (Carol)

SPINACH DIP

1 cup sour cream
1 cup mayonnaise
1 package Knorr vegetable soup mix
4 to 5 green onions, chopped

½ cup chopped water chestnuts
1 package frozen chopped spinach,
  thawed and squeezed dry

Mix all ingredients. Refrigerate for at least 2 hours until flavors blend. Serve with crackers or toast triangles.

Mrs. John Giordano (Mary Alice)

SUPER-SUPER SPINACH VEGETABLE DIP

1 package frozen chopped spinach,
  thawed
2 cups sour cream
2 cups mayonnaise

1 package Knorr vegetable soup
  seasoning
1 red cabbage
Vegetable sticks

Combine spinach, sour cream, mayonnaise and soup seasoning in blender. Pour mixture into red cabbage shell and surround with vegetable sticks. Enjoy.

J. Roger Williams
Williams Chrysler/Plymouth/Imperial

WATER CHESTNUT DIP

1 (8-ounce) can water chestnuts, drained
  and chopped
1 (8-ounce) carton sour cream
1 cup mayonnaise

2 tablespoons soy sauce
3 small green onions, finely chopped
½ cup finely chopped parsley

Mix all ingredients and chill.

Mrs. C. Harold Brown (Carol)

CRAB SPREAD

1 can crab meat, drained, reserving
  juice
1 large package cream cheese
1 teaspoon lemon juice

¼ teaspoon curry powder
1 tablespoon reserved crab juice
1 tablespoon cooking sherry

Mix all ingredients and bake at 350° for 20 to 30 minutes.

Mrs. Charles Stenholm (Cynthia Ann)
Wife, U. S. Congressman

DON MEREDITH'S PIMENTO CHEESE

¼ cup minced green pepper
¼ cup minced onion
½ cup chopped pimento
⅓ cup mayonnaise
1 cup whipped cream cheese

2 tablespoons sherry
1 tablespoon chopped seeded jalapeños
1 large box Velveeta cheese
Dash Worcestershire sauce

Mix all ingredients well. Serve at room temperature with Fritos, crackers or crudités.

Don Meredith
ABC Sports

AVOCADO CHEESE BALL

2 (8-ounce) packages cream cheese,
  softened
1 cup grated sharp Cheddar cheese
1 cup grated mild Cheddar cheese
1 large ripe avocado, mashed
1 medium onion, minced

½ cup finely chopped nuts
2 garlic cloves, minced
1 (4-ounce) can chopped green chilies,
  drained
Fresh parsley, chopped

Mix cheeses well. Mix in avocado, onion, nuts, garlic and green chilies. Adjust seasonings to your taste. Shape into 1 large ball or 2 small balls. Roll in parsley. Serves 20 to 30.

Mrs. J. Herman Musick (Celeste)

PARTY CHEESE BALL

2 (8-ounce) packages cream cheese,
  softened
1 (8-ounce) package sharp Cheddar
  cheese, grated
1 tablespoon chopped pimento
1 tablespoon chopped green pepper

1 tablespoon finely chopped onion
2 teaspoons Worcestershire sauce
Dash cayenne pepper
Dash salt
Pecans, finely chopped

Blend cheeses. Mix in pimento, green pepper, onion, Worcestershire sauce, cayenne pepper and salt. Chill. Shape mixture into a ball and roll in pecans. Serve with crackers and bread.

Nell B. Robinson

BETTY'S CHEESE BALL

½ pound Velveeta
2 jars Old English or Vera sharp cheese
  spread
1 jar Roka or Blue cheese
1 (3-ounce) package cream cheese,
  softened

2 teaspoons onion juice
8 to 10 dashes Worcestershire sauce
Finely chopped pecans

Blend all cheeses with an electric mixer in a small bowl. Add onion juice and Worcestershire sauce. Cover and chill until firm. With buttery hands, turn out on waxed paper and roll in pecans. (This is gooey, but stick with it.) When cheese is covered, shape into a ball and chill until ready to use.

Bud Franks
Casa Manana

RUGELACH

3 cups flour
½ teaspoon baking powder
½ teaspoon salt

2 scant cups vegetable shortening
1 cup orange juice

Sift flour with baking powder and salt. Mix with shortening and orange juice on medium speed of mixer. Wrap dough in waxed paper and refrigerate for several hours or overnight. Separate dough into small sections (about 6 parts.) Working with 1 section at a time, knead with flour. Roll in a circle to ¼-inch thickness (or a little thinner.) Sprinkle with filling mixture and cut into pinwheel pattern (about 20 cookies for each section of dough.) Roll up from outside in. Bake on baking sheet at 350° to 375° for about 20 minutes, or until light golden brown. Makes 110 to 120 cookies.

FILLING

¾ cup sugar
1 teaspoon cinnamon

½ cup chopped nuts

Mix all ingredients.

"Butch" Luskey
Luskey's Western Stores

EGG ROLLS

½ pound cooked shrimp, diced
½ pound ground pork, beef or veal,
  cooked
1 cup finely chopped celery
½ cup coarsely chopped water chestnuts
½ cup chopped fresh green onion
2 teaspoons salt
1 teaspoon sugar

⅛ teaspoon black pepper
¼ teaspoon Worcestershire sauce
⅛ teaspoon dark Oriental seasoning
1½ tablespoons butter, melted
1 egg, well-beaten
1 tablespoon peanut butter
Egg roll wrappers
Peanut oil

Working with your hands, mix shrimp, meat, celery, water chestnuts, green onion, salt, sugar, black pepper, Worcestershire sauce, Oriental seasoning, butter and egg. Mix in peanut butter last. Roll into egg roll wrappers. (Size of egg rolls will depend on size of wrappers.) Heat peanut oil to 360° and fry egg rolls until golden brown. Note: This recipe comes from a Chinese-American and is the real thing.

David Lehmann (Wendy)
Real Estate/Investments

PICKLED SHRIMP

2 tablespoons olive oil
1 pound shrimp with tails, cooked and
  cleaned
1 cup white vinegar
2 tablespoons water
½ cup paper-thin white onion slices

8 whole cloves
1 bay leaf
2 teaspoons salt
1 teaspoon sugar
Dash cayenne pepper

Dribble the oil over the shrimp. Mix remaining ingredients in a saucepan, bring to a boil and pour over shrimp and olive oil while hot. Cook and then refrigerate for at least 48 hours.

River Crest Country Club

SHRIMP COCKTAIL

Frozen raw shrimp
1 tablespoon salt

2 tablespoons vinegar

Drop shrimp in vigorously boiling water in a large kettle to which salt and vinegar have been added. Cover, bring quickly to a boil again, and cook 2 minutes. Remove immediately from water. Cover with ice to cool. Peel and devein. Serve with 1 of the following sauces.

REMOULADE SAUCE

1 cup mayonnaise
2 anchovy fillets, chopped
½ teaspoon dry mustard
1 tablespoon wine vinegar
1 tablespoon tarragon vinegar

2 tablespoons dry sherry
½ cup chopped parsley
¼ teaspoon garlic powder
4 tablespoons capers
1 tablespoon onion juice

Mix all ingredients. Yields 1½ cups.

COCKTAIL SAUCE

1 cup catsup
1 cup chili sauce

2 to 4 tablespoons horseradish
4 tablespoons lemon juice

Mix all ingredients.

Nell B. Robinson

VENISON OR BEEF JERKY

3 pounds lean beef or venison
¾ tablespoon salt
1 teaspoon onion powder
1 teaspoon garlic powder
1 teaspoon Accent

½ teaspoon pepper
⅓ cup Worcestershire sauce
¼ cup soy sauce
1 teaspoon Liquid Smoke

Semi-freeze and slice meat ¼-inch thick. Mix remaining ingredients and marinate overnight. Drain and pat dry. Prepare in dehydrator or on racks in oven at 200° for approximately 12 hours.

Darla Tinsley
Gaylen's Bar-BQ

LBJ Ranch

Stonewall, Texas

Mrs. Lyndon B. Johnson's recipe for

Spice Tea

6 teaspoons tea (or 8 teabags)
2 cups boiling water

Pour water over tea and let cool. Strain and add:

1 small can frozen lemon juice
1 small can frozen orange juice
1 1/2 cups sugar
2 quarts water
1 stick of cinnamon

Simmer mixture for 20 minutes. If too strong, add water.
Add extra sugar to taste. This recipe makes 16 to 20 cups.

I like to serve this
to guests on a cold winter's
day here at the Ranch —
just as I did at the White
House — Lady Bird Johnson

APERITIF CHICKEN NECK WHOOPEE

Pour 2 gallons of rum (or Scotch or bourbon or beer or vodka or any mixture thereof) into large container with strong handles. For hint of flavor, pass 6 boiled chicken necks over the liquid while making certain these never actually touch other ingredients. Next, throw chicken necks in garbage or feed to your cat. Drink remaining liquids after carefully hiding car keys and disconnecting telephone.

Larry L. King
Author
"The Best Little Whorehouse in Texas"

TAYLOR FAMILY CHRISTMAS EGGNOG

12 eggs, separated
12 tablespoons sugar
2 cups bourbon

1 pint heavy cream
Nutmeg
1 cup milk

Beat egg yolks, add sugar and mix well. Stir in the bourbon. Beat egg whites until stiff. Whip cream until stiff. Fold whipped cream and egg whites into yolk mixture. Sprinkle with nutmeg. Note: To thin, add milk or more bourbon. Serves 18.

Susan C. Taylor
Daughter, Mayor of Dallas, Texas

CAPPUCCINO

2 cups coffee
2 cups nonfat dry milk
1 tablespoon sugar

1 tablespoon cocoa
1 shot brandy
Whipped cream

Mix coffee, dry milk, sugar, cocoa and brandy in a saucepan and bring to a boil. Top with whipped cream to serve. Serves 4.

Nell B. Robinson

THE 46-OUNCE "STORMIN' NORMAN" SPECIAL

After consuming this, you will be "Stormin'", too!

Ice
4 ounces light rum
Orange juice

Sweet and sour
Grenadine

Fill a 46-ounce glass full of ice. Add the rum and equal parts of orange juice and sweet and sour. For red color, add grenadine until you've got a super-colored drink.

"Stormin' Norman" Nazar

ROMAN PUNCH

1 pound medium brown sugar
Juice of 3 oranges
Juice of 6 lemons
4 dashes angostura bitters
6 egg whites, beaten to a stiff froth

1 quart light rum, chilled
1 block ice
1 quart champagne, chilled
1 quart sparkling water, chilled

Dissolve brown sugar with orange juice, lemon juice and bitters. Add beaten egg whites; mix well. Stir in rum. Add block of ice. Just before serving, add champagne and sparkling water. Serves 25 (4-ounce) glasses. Note: This punch is sneaky; have non-drinkers or taxis on call! To extend formula, double amount of juices and increase sparkling water to 2 or even 3 quarts. To avoid sticky fingers, lips, and utensils, omit egg whites, which are for appearance only.

Bob Horan
1981-82 State President
Texas Restaurant Assn.

MUD FLAP

1 ounce Kahlua
1 ounce Peppermint Schnapps

Cream

In Collins glass, combine ingredients. Stir well.

Pam and Kathy
Oui Lounge

CONFEDERATE HOME BREWED GINGER BEER

1 pint molasses
2 spoonfuls ginger
Boiling water

Cold water
1 pint yeast

Mix molasses and ginger in a 2 gallon pail. Fill halfway with boiling water. Stir to mix well. Fill pail with cold water, leaving room for the yeast. (The yeast must not be added until the mixture is lukewarm.) Stir in yeast. Place pail on a warm hearth for the night. Bottle in the morning. May be drinkable in 24 hours.

Jim Marrs
Journalist

MY FAVORITE FRUIT SMOOTHIE
Fruit/diet for high energy breakfast.
(Especially for news anchors.)

1 banana, frozen
½ cup strawberries
1 ripe peach
½ cup apple juice

3 tablespoons plain yogurt
3 tablespoons protein powder
Honey or Sweet & Low, to taste
4 ice cubes

Combine ingredients in blender. Blend well.

Linda Schaefer
News Anchor
KTBC-TV
Austin, Texas

COFFEE PUNCH

¼ cup instant coffee
½ cup sugar
2 quarts water
2 cups cold milk

2 teaspoons vanilla
1 quart vanilla ice cream
1 cup whipping cream, whipped
Nutmeg

Blend instant coffee with sugar. Add water and stir until coffee and sugar are dissolved. Stir in milk and vanilla, and chill the mixture thoroughly. Just before serving, place partially softened ice cream into chilled bowl. Pour coffee mixture over ice cream. Top with whipped cream and sprinkle lightly with nutmeg. Serves 15 to 18.

Nell B. Robinson

FRUIT PUNCH

3½ cups sugar
1 pint strong hot tea
2 cups lemon juice
3 quarts orange juice or 2 (12-ounce)
  cans frozen orange juice concentrate,
  diluted 3 parts water to 1 part
  orange

1 (46-ounce) can pineapple juice
3 quarts ice water
1 quart ginger ale, chilled
Orange, lemon, pineapple or strawberry
  slices, to garnish

Dissolve sugar in hot tea. Mix with juices and ice water. Chill. At serving time, add chilled ginger ale. Serve punch well chilled. Float orange slices, lemon slices, fresh pineapple or fresh strawberry slices in punch. Makes 2 gallons or 50 servings.

Carol Davis

HOT CRANBERRY PUNCH

1 cup brown sugar
3¾ cups water
9 cups unsweetened pineapple juice
9 cups cranberry juice cocktail

4 cinnamon sticks
4½ teaspoons whole cloves
½ teaspoon salt

Mix all ingredients and perk in electric percolator. Makes 32 (4-ounce) servings.

Nell B. Robinson

ALMOND TEA

4 small tea bags
2½ cups boiling water
4 cups water
1 cup sugar

½ cup fresh lemon juice
1 teaspoon almond extract
½ teaspoon vanilla extract

Steep tea bags in boiling water for 5 minutes. Mix remaining water with sugar and boil for 5 minutes. Combine liquids. Stir in lemon juice, almond extract and vanilla extract. Chill overnight. Heat to serve. This tea must be made the day before serving.

Mrs. J. Herman Musick (Celeste)

Cattle and windmills conjure up as many visions of Texas as do the Alamo and oil wells. Cattle were first brought to Texas by Spanish soldiers and priests who came to establish missions in the late seventeenth century, and by the middle 1700's, a thriving cattle culture had grown up in the brush country of South Texas. After the extermination of the buffalo and the removal of the Indians from the high plains of Texas, the cattle culture spread north and west. The lack of water in West Texas led to the development of the wind-driven water pumps in the 1870's and 1880's. This introduction allowed men like Charles Goodnight, Samuel Burk Burnett, and W. T. Waggoner, who had pioneered ranching on the high plains, to refine their techniques and shape the cattle industry into the multi-billion dollar endeavor it has become today.

dallas cowboys football club

CORNBREAD MUFFINS

1-1/4 cups cornmeal

1 teaspoon salt

2 Tablespoons baking powder

2 cups milk

3/4 cup flour

1/2 Tablespoon sugar

2 small eggs

2 Tablespoons shortening

Sift dry ingredients. Beat eggs well. Add a little more than half of the milk to the eggs and beat well. Add egg mixture to flour mixture and beat well. Stir in rest of milk and melted shortening. Fill hot, well-greased muffin tins about half full. Bake at 500° for about 15 - 18 minutes. Makes 12 muffins.

(A favorite cornbread recipe of Mr. Tom Landry, Head Coach, Dallas Cowboys.)

ROY BLAKE
State Senator

Committees:

Chairman:
ADMINISTRATION

Member:
FINANCE
STATE AFFAIRS
SUBCOMMITTEE ON
NOMINATIONS

Dear Russell:

Enclosed please find a favorite receipe of mine
for Crusty Potato Pancakes.

I hope that this is helpful to you in your book.

Sincerely,

Senator Roy Blake
District 3

**The Senate of
The State of Texas
Austin 78711**

ROY BLAKE
State Senator

Committees:

Chairman:
ADMINISTRATION

Member:
FINANCE
STATE AFFAIRS
SUBCOMMITTEE ON
NOMINATIONS

Crusty Potato Pancakes

6 medium potatoes, peeled
1 small onion, grated
3 eggs
3/4 cup flour
2 teaspoons salt
Oil for frying

Grate potatoes coarsely into a bowl filled with cold water.
This keeps the potatoes from turning dark and removes
some of the excess starch, making the pancakes crisper.
In another bowl, combine the onion, eggs, flour and salt.
Drain potatoes, pressing out all liquid. Beat potatoes into
batter. Heat oil. Spoon heaping tablespoons of batter into
oil, spreading batter with back of spoon into 4 - inch rounds.
Brown on 1 side, turn and brown on the other side. Brown
the pancakes slowly so potatoes will have a chance to cook
through properly. Drain on absorbent paper. Serve hot
with applesauce.

Roy Blake

SALADO   TEXAS

Hush Puppies

2 cups corn meal
1 teaspoon baking powder
3 tablespoons sugar
1/4 cup butter
1 tablespoon salt

Combine meal, baking powder, sugar and salt. Add
slowly to 3 1/2 cups boiling water, stirring briskly.
As soon as mixture is smooth, remove from heat.
Stir in butter, cool. Form into finger shaped rolls.
Fry in 2 inches hot fat, 375 degrees, until golden
brown. Drain on absorbent paper. Makes about three
dozen.

AS FEATURED IN   LIFE   Ford TIMES   TIME
May 15, 1963

ALMOND FRENCH TOAST

10 ounces almonds
5 ounces honey
2 or more teaspoons cinnamon
1 can evaporated milk
1 loaf extra thin white bread slices
(Pepperidge Farm)

½ pound butter, melted
4 eggs
Vanilla, to taste
Almond extract, to taste

Process almonds, honey and cinnamon in a blender. Add evaporated milk to thin. Use this as sandwich filling on bread slices. Brush both sides with melted butter. Mix remaining butter, eggs, vanilla and almond extract. Dip sandwiches in egg batter like French toast. Broil about 3 minutes, turn and broil second side. Freeze or serve immediately with syrup.

Paula Zahn
News Anchor
KRPC-TV
Houston, Texas
* Paula Zahn has moved to WNEV-TV, Boston

BANANA NUT BREAD

½ cup margarine
1 cup sugar
2 eggs
½ teaspoon salt
1 teaspoon vanilla

1 teaspoon soda
2 cups flour
3 bananas, mashed
½ cup chopped nuts

Cream margarine and sugar. Beat in eggs, salt and vanilla. Sift soda with flour and add, mixing thoroughly. Stir in bananas and nuts. Pour into greased loaf pan. Bake at 300° for 1 hour or until done.

Mrs. Bill Sarpalius (Donna)
Wife, State Senator

MY FAVORITE MUFFINS

½ cup butter (no substitute)
1 cup brown sugar
1 cup sour milk or buttermilk
1 teaspoon soda
1 egg
2 cups all-purpose flour

1 teaspoon vanilla
1 teaspoon cinnamon
1 teaspoon cloves
1 teaspoon mace
½ cup mixed dates, cherries and pecans

Mix ingredients in order given, beating with a wooden spoon after each addition. Fill muffin tin cups and bake at 400° for 20 minutes or until lightly browned. Note: Mace is important to the recipe, so do not leave it out. You may use any choice of fruits or nuts (½ cup total), but if you don't have any, I like it plain, too. I often ice the muffins with powdered sugar icing. Melt some butter, add powdered sugar, and thin with hot coffee.

Mrs. Al Salley (Shirley)

APPLESAUCE CUPCAKES

½ cup margarine
1 egg
¼ cup sugar
1½ cups flour, sifted
1 teaspoon soda
¼ teaspoon salt

1 teaspoon cinnamon
1½ teaspoons nutmeg
1 cup unsweetened applesauce
1 teaspoon vanilla
¼ cup chopped walnuts or pecans
4 teaspoons raisins

Preheat oven to 375°. Cream margarine until fluffy. Beat egg with sugar and blend with margarine mixture. Sift together the flour, soda, salt, cinnamon and nutmeg. Add to margarine mixture alternately with applesauce, mixing well after each addition. Stir in vanilla, nuts and raisins. Spoon into 12 muffin tin cups which have been sprayed with vegetable pan spray. Bake for 15 to 20 minutes. Yields 12 cupcakes. Note: Exchange per cupcake is ½ bread, 2 fat and 1 fruit. Estimated nutrients per serving are: CAL - 174; CHO - 18; PRO - 3; FAT - 10; Na - 239; and K - 52.

Doyle Willis
State Representative

OLD-FASHIONED GINGERBREAD WITH LEMON SAUCE

½ cup butter or margarine
½ cup sugar
1 egg
1 cup dark cane syrup
2½ cups flour, sifted
1½ teaspoons soda
1 teaspoon cinnamon
1 teaspoon ginger

½ teaspoon nutmeg
¼ teaspoon cloves
½ teaspoon salt
1 cup boiling water
3 tablespoons preserved (crystallized)
    ginger, finely chopped
1 cup chopped pecans (optional)

Cream butter, sugar and egg. Add syrup. Sift flour, soda, cinnamon, ginger, nutmeg, cloves and salt and add to first mixture. Beat well. Add boiling water, ginger and nuts. Grease and lightly flour a 14x10-inch baking pan. Pour in mixture and bake at 350° for about 25 minutes. When done, cut in generous squares. Pour lemon sauce over squares to serve.

LEMON SAUCE
2 eggs
¾ cup sugar
2 tablespoons flour
Juice of 2 lemons

⅛ teaspoon lemon rind
Pinch salt
2 tablespoons butter
1 cup very hot water

Mix all ingredients except hot water in a saucepan. (An electric blender does this trick in an instant.) When ingredients are well-mixed, add hot water. Stir well and cook until thick, but do not boil. Note: For variation, omit the lemon juice and add a little nutmeg and cinnamon.

Allan Shivers
Governor of Texas
1949-1957

CHEESE BISCUITS

2 sticks margarine or butter
2 cups flour
2 cups grated extra sharp cheese

2 cups Rice Krispies
Salt, to taste
12 to 15 drops Tabasco sauce, or more

Melt margarine or butter, add flour and cheese. Mix in Rice Krispies, salt and Tabasco sauce. Roll into tiny balls. Freeze. Bake on ungreased cookie sheet at 400° for 20 minutes.

Margaret Lowdon

MACK WALLACE'S BISCUITS

Biscuits-The basic recipe is available to anyone with a good cookbook. Making biscuits is a matter of mental attitude, determination and practice.

First, there is a belief that "I can make as good damn biscuits as anyone!" If you don't believe this, stop now.

Second, equipment: (1) an oven with a reasonably good temperature gauge, (2) a baking pan-black and just a little beat up-about 8 or 9 inches square or similar size round, and (3) flour, buttermilk, salt, sugar, baking powder, shortening (Crisco).

The night before put buttermilk out to come to room temperature. This is important-cold milk does not act as fast with the baking powder. If you have forgotten this, don't despair-put 1¼ cups buttermilk in microwave approximately 45 seconds on *high*. Whey will separate and it will lump up-that's OK.

Preheat oven to 450°-475°.

Mix 2 cups flour, 5 teaspoons baking powder, ½ teaspoon salt, 2 teaspoons sugar in a mixing bowl. Stir up good with a fork. I have sifted *once, twice,* and *not at all* and can't tell the difference.

Here put in ¼ cup or tiny bit more Crisco shortening and mix well. I have used one of those cutting tools, a fork or my bare hands when nothing else is available for mixing.

Pour a little Wesson oil or equivalent in baking pan. You don't have time to do this after you cut the biscuits.

Put out a sheet of waxed paper about 24 inches long. Sprinkle flour on waxed paper. If you don't get enough flour here a disaster occurs. It has a tendency to stick to paper.

Now dump the buttermilk in the mixing bowl and stir flour and milk together with fork being careful to mix well-a ball of dough should form. It will be sticky. Sprinkle a little flour on ball of dough till you can sort of round it into a ball. Put this ball of dough on the floured waxed paper and work it a time or two. Then pat it out in a round shape to about ½ inch thick. I use a glass or biscuit cutter and cut it into biscuits. Take tails and hand-make 2 or 3 more biscuits. Depending on size of cutter, this recipe makes 12 to 20 biscuits.

Take pan with oil in it and dip a little oil on top and bottom of biscuit and place in pan until it is filled.

Pop in oven for 10 to 12 minutes, depending on oven.

Sometimes bottoms brown first. (It all depends on rack and oven characteristics. Should be in middle or just a little above.) In event bottoms brown first, turn on broiler for 30 to 40 seconds-*tops* will brown.

If you like thick biscuits, squeeze together in pan. If you like thin, spread out. My grandmother using this recipe made the best I have ever eaten in a wood cookstove without a thermostat. My mother still uses this recipe and 7 or 8 years ago I asked her to teach me so that it would not be forgotten.

Mack Wallace
Chairman, Texas Railroad Commission

ORANGE BISCUITS

2 cups all-purpose flour, sifted
4 tablespoons sugar
1 teaspoon salt
2½ teaspoons baking powder

4 tablespoons shortening
Grated rind of 1 orange
¾ cup liquid (half milk, half orange
  juice)

Sift together flour, sugar, salt and baking powder. Cut in shortening until the size of small peas. Mix in rind and all liquid at 1 time. Mix lightly just to blend. Knead lightly on a floured surface 8 to 10 times. Roll out on floured board ½-inch thick. Cut into rounds with floured 2-inch cutters. Place close together on ungreased cookie sheet and bake at 450° for 12 to 15 minutes, until golden brown. Makes 12 high biscuits.

Mrs. John B. Connally (Nellie)
Wife, Governor of Texas
1962-1968

CHEESE CORN BREAD

1 cup yellow cornmeal
1 cup all-purpose flour, sifted
¼ cup sugar
½ teaspoon salt
4 teaspoons baking powder

1½ cups grated sharp Cheddar cheese
1 egg
1 cup milk
¼ cup shortening, softened

Sift together cornmeal, flour, sugar, salt and baking powder. Stir in cheese. Mix in egg, milk and shortening. Beat with a rotary beater about 1 minute or until smooth. Do not overbeat. Pour in a greased 8-inch square pan. Bake at 375° for 30 minutes. Cut in squares. Serve hot. Serves 8.

Allan Shivers
Governor of Texas
1949-1957

THE BIG PANCAKE
Texas-size, one might say.

1⅛ cups Bisquick mix
½ cup buttermilk
⅛ cup oil

⅛ cup honey (preferably buckwheat
   flavor)
1 egg white

Heat oven to 425°. Grease an 11x7-inch pan. Combine all ingredients and mix until blended. Spread batter evenly into prepared pan. Bake 10 to 15 minutes. Cut into serving pieces. Serve with butter, jelly, syrup or honey. Serves 2 to 4. Note: Recipe can be doubled using 1 whole egg and baked in a 15x10-inch jellyroll pan.

Jim Blue
News Anchor
KAMR-TV
Amarillo, Texas

TAVERN BREAD

3 cups self-rising flour
½ cup sugar

1 cup beer, at room temperature (not
   light beer)
¼ pound butter, melted

Preheat oven to 350°. Mix flour and sugar. Add beer and mix well. Spoon into a greased 9x5-inch loaf pan. Bake at 350° for 45 minutes. Remove from oven and pour melted butter over the loaf. Return to oven for 15 minutes. This can be frozen and reheated before serving.

Margaret Lowdon

TRINITY ROLLS

1 cup self-rising flour
1 stick butter, very soft (no substitute)

1 small carton sour cream

Mix ingredients well. Bake in paper-lined muffin tin at 375° for 20 minutes or until lightly browned. Makes 8.

Barry Bailey
First Methodist Church
Fort Worth, Texas

The State Fair of Texas was begun in the late 1800's by a group of Dallas businessmen eager to show the accomplishments of the community. In 1903, the City of Dallas purchased the State Fair and the 277 acres of what is now Fair Park. The State Fair offers midway rides and exhibits, a rodeo, a car show, a Broadway show, and it is the battleground of the annual Texas-Oklahoma football game. In the past, the State Fair has drawn crowds of three million people. For the 1986 Sesquicentennial celebration, the State Fair plans to run 52 days in honor of Texas' 150th birthday.

(Source: State Fair of Texas)

Dallas Country Club

DCC Gumbo (10 portions)

2 celery hearts
2 bell peppers   chop into 3/4 inch pieces
2 white onions
6 whole tomatoes, peeled; seeded, and cut into large pieces
1 small can tomato paste
1 pinch rosemary
1 pinch thyme
1 1/2 teaspoons gumbo file powder (if stronger gumbo taste
   is desired use more file)
salt and pepper to taste
dash of tabasco (optional)
2 1/2 quarts fish stock
1 cup vegetable oil
2 cups fresh okra
1 cup cooked rice
Seafood such as cod, red snapper, red fish, white and shrimp
Roux for thickening of soup (Roux - mixture of 1 cup flour and
   3/4 cup oil

Saute celery, onion and peppers in vegetable oil, add tomatoes,
tomato paste and spices. Add fish stock and let simmer for 5 -
10 minutes. Blend the freshly cut okra to the simmering broth
(the starch from the okra will slightly thicken the stock; if a
slightly heavier soup is desired use a little Roux) Last, add the
remaining ingredients; fish, shrimp and rice.

CARDIOVASCULAR ASSOCIATES
TEXAS HEART INSTITUTE

Dear Mr. Gardner:

Thank you for your letter of April 10, 1984. Enclosed are two recipes which have been favorites in our home. I hope that you will be able to use one or both of them.

With best wishes for success with your project, I am

Sincerely yours,

Denton A. Cooley, M.D.

DAC:jm
enclosures

GAZPACHO

```
1    clove garlic
3    pounds tomatoes
2    cucumbers
½    cup minced green pepper
½    cup minced onion
2    cups iced tomato juice
1/3 cup olive oil
3    tablesponns vinegar
Salt and freshly ground pepper
¼    teaspoon Tabasco
avocado slices
```

Chop garlic very fine, add to a large bowl with peeled, seeded and
chopped tomatoes. (Try to save as much of the juice as you can.)
Peel and seed the cucumbers and add to the bowl with the pepper, onion,
and tomato juice. Add the olive oil and seasonings, cover and chill
thoroughly.   Taste for seasoning - more garlic is usually complementary.
Serve in chilled bowls with ice cube of frozen tomato juice and an
avocado slice

Denton A. Cooley, M.D.
Surgeon-in-Chief
Texas Heart Institute
Houston, Texas

MARVIN LEATH
11TH DISTRICT, TEXAS

Congress of the United States
House of Representatives
Washington, D.C.

ARMED SERVICES COMMITTEE
SUBCOMMITTEES:
PROCUREMENT AND
MILITARY NUCLEAR SYSTEMS
READINESS

VETERANS' AFFAIRS COMMITTEE
SUBCOMMITTEES:
CHAIRMAN,
HOUSING AND MEMORIAL AFFAIRS
EDUCATION, TRAINING AND
EMPLOYMENT
OVERSIGHT AND INVESTIGATIONS

Dear Russell:

Thank you for your note requesting a recipe for the book you are working on. I am glad to contribute one of my favorites which is for Potato Soup.

Good luck on your project and thanks for wanting to include me.

Yours very truly,

Marvin Leath
Congressman

ML:jcj

Enclosure

MARVIN LEATH
11TH DISTRICT, TEXAS

Congress of the United States
House of Representatives
Washington, D.C.

ARMED SERVICES COMMITTEE
SUBCOMMITTEES:
PROCUREMENT AND
MILITARY NUCLEAR SYSTEMS
READINESS

VETERANS' AFFAIRS COMMITTEE
SUBCOMMITTEES:
CHAIRMAN,
HOUSING AND MEMORIAL AFFAIRS
EDUCATION, TRAINING AND
EMPLOYMENT
OVERSIGHT AND INVESTIGATIONS

POTATO SOUP

6	medium potatoes, diced
2	medium onions, diced
1/2	cup chopped celery
2	quarts water
1/2	teaspoon coarse black pepper
	salt to taste
2	tablespoons flour
2	tablespoons butter
1	cup cream
1/2	cup fresh parsley
1/2	teaspoon dill seed, ground

Boil potatoes, onions and celery
in water until tender. Remove
vegetables, reserving broth. Blend
vegetables in blender or force
through sieve. Return to broth.
Add pepper, salt, flour and butter
to cream and stir into soup. Stir
in parsley and dill. Reheat to
serving temperature, but do not boil.
Makes 6 to 8 servings and may be
frozen.

                Congressman Marvin Leath
                Texas 11th District

Sopa de Xochicalpan

This is a soup inspired by Ancient Aztec cooking. The word Xochicalpan in the language of Nahuatl (Aztec) means the place of the house of flowers. It has an aroma that is almost a fragrance.

Ingredients

2 large chicken breasts, boiled and shredded into bite-sized pieces

2 cans chicken broth or stock and water

1 small white onion finely chopped

1 tomato peeled, seeded and coarsely chopped

$\frac{1}{2}$ Bell pepper chopped

1 corn tortilla julienned into 1" x 1/4" slices

1 lime cut into thin ($\frac{1}{8}$") slices

$\frac{1}{2}$ tsp. Red Wine Vinegar

Seasonings

Garlic powder

$\frac{1}{8}$ tsp. ground coriander seeds

$\frac{1}{4}$ tsp. ground cumin seeds

black pepper to taste

Preparation

Using an enamel soup pot, pour in the stock and water. Add the chopped white onion, the tomato, & green pepper. Add the Vinegar and the dry seasonings and simmer until vegetables are cooked.

add the chicken and simmer while the flavors combine. Add the tortilla strips.

To Serve

Place a slice of lime in each bowl and ladle the soup over it. Wait a moment for the lime to flavor the soup. Then serve.

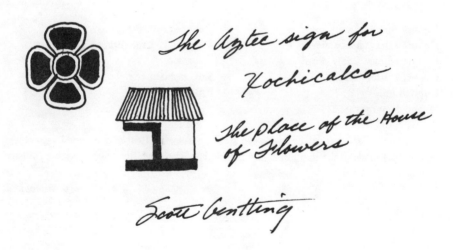

The Aztec sign for

Xochicalco

The place of the House of Flowers

Scott Gentling

CREAM OF ALMOND SOUP

1 celery stalk, minced
1 garlic clove, peeled and pressed
2 tablespoons butter
3 cups chicken broth
⅔ cup finely ground blanched almonds

⅛ teaspoon mace
1 cup heavy cream
1 to 2 tablespoons toasted almonds, to
   garnish

Stir-fry celery and garlic in butter until limp. Add broth, ground almonds and mace. Cover and simmer for 30 to 40 minutes, stirring occasionally. Remove from heat and let stand 1 hour. Puree in blender or pass through sieve. Return mixture to pan, add cream and heat, uncovered, for 2 to 3 minutes. Do not boil. Season to taste and serve hot or cold garnished with toasted almonds.

Mrs. Gary Cook
Wife, Mayor of Wichita Falls, Texas

CHEESE SOUP

1 quart carrots, finely diced
1 quart celery, finely diced
1 quart onions, finely diced
1 quart chicken stock
1 gallon milk
⅔ pound margarine

7 ounces cornstarch
4½ pounds Kraft Ribbon Slice Cheese,
   grated
Salt, to taste
Pepper, to taste

Cook carrots, celery and onions in chicken stock until tender. Heat milk and add vegetables. Add a paste made of the margarine and cornstarch. Slowly add the cheese. Season to taste with salt and pepper.

C. A. Sanford
C.A.'s Restaurant
1983-84 State President
Texas Restaurant Assn.

AVOCADO SHERRY BISQUE

2 tablespoons butter
1 small onion, diced
2 tablespoons flour
3 cups fresh chicken stock
1 tablespoon fresh lemon juice
½ cup Christian Brothers Cocktail
   Sherry

2 garlic cloves, pressed
1 teaspoon salt
½ teaspoon black pepper
2 ripe avocados, diced
2 cups half-and-half
Parsley, chopped
Fresh tomatoes, chopped

Melt butter in a large saucepan. Sauté onion until soft. Stir in flour. Add chicken stock and cook until thick. Stir in lemon juice, sherry, garlic, salt and pepper, and simmer for 15 minutes. Blend diced avocados with half-and-half until smooth. Add to saucepan and simmer for 10 minutes. Chill and serve garnished with chopped parsley. Or serve hot, garnished with chopped tomatoes.

Ray Underwood

CREAMY CHICKEN & MUSHROOM SOUP

½ pound mushrooms
¼ cup chopped onion
Butter
2 cups cooked chicken

2 cans cream of mushroom soup
2 cups milk
1½ cups noodles

Sauté mushrooms and onion in butter until tender. Add chicken, mushroom soup, milk and noodles. Simmer slowly for 30 minutes. Add more milk if the soup becomes too thick.

Mrs. Mickey Leland (Alison Walton)
Wife, U. S. Congressman

BEER CHEESE SOUP

2 cups milk
1 can flat beer, room temperature
1 can chicken broth
1 (16-ounce) jar Cheez Whiz

White pepper, to taste
Worcestershire sauce, to taste
Tabasco sauce, to taste
Chopped chives, to garnish

Combine milk, beer, broth and cheese in a saucepan. Heat, stirring constantly. Season to desired taste. Sprinkle with chopped chives.

Lee Angle

CORN CHOWDER

3 large potatoes, peeled and cubed
1 tablespoon salt
1 (8-ounce) can creamed corn
2 onion slices
2 ounces butter

1 large can evaporated milk
2 cups whole milk
Butter
Salt, to taste
Pepper, to taste

In large pot cover potatoes with water, add 1 tablespoon salt and bring to a boil. Let boil for 10 minutes. Add creamed corn to mixture. In a separate pan, sauté onion in butter. Then add that plus evaporated milk and whole milk to potato mixture. Let boil. Season with additional butter, salt and pepper, to taste.

Bill Scanlon

PUMPKIN ALMOND BISQUE IN ITS OWN SHELL
First Place Award–Gourmet Gala, Houston, Texas 1983

1 pumpkin
2 tablespoons butter
3 tablespoons chopped celery
3 tablespoons chopped onion
2 cups cooked pumpkin purée
1 tablespoon tomato paste
2 tablespoons almond paste

3 cups chicken broth
1½ cups light cream
1 teaspoon nutmeg
1 teaspoon white pepper
Salt, to taste
3 tablespoons Amaretto
Toasted pumpkin seeds, to garnish

Remove flesh from pumpkin, cutting so that the shell can be reserved as a serving container. Simmer flesh in small amount of stock until tender. Purée in blender. Melt butter in heavy pan, add celery and onion and simmer for 5 minutes. Add to pumpkin in blender along with tomato paste and almond paste. Blend until smooth, return to pot with chicken broth and simmer for 30 minutes. Blend the cream into the soup and cook until hot. Season with nutmeg, pepper, salt and Amaretto. Serve in pumpkin shell and float toasted pumpkin seeds on each serving. This recipe is from my book, *The Compleat Pumpkin Eater*, and is served at the Remington on Post Oak in Houston and at The Mansion on Turtle Creek in Dallas.

Mrs. Caroline Hunt Schoellkopf

MY VERY OWN COLD TOMATO SOUP
This is great!

3 cans Campbell's tomato soup
3 cans milk or half-and-half
6 tablespoons finely chopped celery

4 tablespoons finely chopped onion
1 teaspoon soy sauce
Fresh limes

Mix soup, milk, celery, onion and soy sauce. Chill. Just before serving, add a good squeeze of fresh lime juice to each chilled soup cup.

Electra Waggoner Biggs
W. T. Waggoner Estate

LEMON SOUP

6 cups fresh chicken broth
¼ cup long grain rice
1 teaspoon salt

3 eggs
¼ cup or more lemon juice
1 lemon, thinly sliced

Combine chicken broth, rice and salt in a large saucepan. Bring to a boil, then reduce heat. Cover and simmer until the rice is just tender. Remove from heat. In a bowl, beat eggs until fluffy and pale yellow, then beat in lemon juice. Slowly stir about 1 cup of hot broth into egg-lemon mixture. Gradually add more. Then pour this into broth. Whisk it until slightly thickened. Cool to room temperature. Refrigerate until icy cold. It will thicken and settle. Before serving, whisk again. Garnish with lemon slices. (I use soup bowls which have been in freezer.)

Ray Underwood

ONION WINE SOUP

¼ cup butter
5 large onions, chopped
5 cups beef broth
½ cup celery leaves
1 large potato, sliced
1 cup dry white wine

1 tablespoon vinegar
2 teaspoons sugar
1 cup light cream
1 tablespoon minced parsley
Salt, to taste
Pepper, to taste

Melt butter in a large saucepan. Add chopped onions and mix well. Add beef broth, celery leaves and potato. Bring to boiling. Cover and simmer for 30 minutes. Purée mixture in a blender. Return to saucepan and blend in wine, vinegar and sugar. Bring to boiling and simmer for 5 minutes. Stir in cream, parsley, salt and pepper. Heat thoroughly but do not boil. Yields 6 to 8 servings.

Nancy Reagan
First Lady of the United States

BARBECUE SAUCE

1 (8-ounce) can tomato juice
¼ cup vinegar
⅓ cup packed brown sugar
½ cup chopped onion

1 garlic clove, minced
2 tablespoons mustard
2 tablespoons chili powder
2 tablespoons dill pickle juice

Mix ingredients in a saucepan. Bring to a boil and simmer for 5 minutes.

Debbie Pennebacker

DAD'S BARBECUE SAUCE

3 cups water
1 cup tomato catsup
1 small can tomato paste
¼ cup vinegar
1 teaspoon sugar
2 teaspoons chili powder
1 teaspoon salt
1 teaspoon black pepper

2 teaspoons paprika
2 garlic cloves, chopped
2 tablespoons chopped onion
2 tablespoons Worcestershire sauce
4 tablespoons butter and oil
½ lemon (squeeze and use rind in
sauce)

Mix ingredients in a saucepan, bring to a boil and let simmer for 20 minutes.

Robert N. Baird
Mrs. Baird's Bakeries

FRANK'S BARBECUE SAUCE

1 cup tomato catsup
½ cup cider vinegar
1 teaspoon sugar
1 teaspoon chili powder
⅛ teaspoon salt
1½ cups water
3 celery stalks, chopped

3 bay leaves
1 garlic clove
2 tablespoons chopped onion
4 tablespoons butter
1 teaspoon paprika
4 tablespoons Worcestershire sauce
Dash black pepper

Bring ingredients to a boil. Simmer for 15 minutes. Remove from heat and strain.

Frank Windegger
Athletic Director
Texas Christian University

DEAR RUSSELL,

I AM HONORED TO BE INCLUDED IN YOUR RECIPE BOOK AMONG SUCH DISTINGUISHED PEOPLE. THIS RECIPE IS OVER 100 YEARS OLD. IT CAME FROM MY GRANDMOTHER, OLA SASSE WARREN, WHO GREW UP IN CENTRAL TEXAS AND LIVED IN DALLAS FOR YEARS. THE COMBINATION OF GRAPES AND GARLIC SOUNDS A BIT UNUSUAL I KNOW, BUT TRY IT. IT'S ABSOLUTELY GREAT.

"GREEN GRAPE DELIGHT"

1 - 3 OZ PKG CREAM CHEESE

1 TBL MAYONNAISE

1 TBL SUGAR

DASH CAYENNE PEPPER

DASH GARLIC POWDER (OR RUB BOWL WITH GARLIC)

2 LBS (4 CUPS) SEEDLESS GREEN GRAPES, HALVED

1 CUP CHOPPED PECANS

COMBINE FIRST FIVE INGREDIENTS AND MIX UNTIL SMOOTH. GENTLY FOLD IN GRAPES AND NUTS. CHILL THOROUGHLY, ABOUT TWO HOURS. SERVE ON LETTUCE LEAVES. SERVES 4 - 6.

IT'S A SIMPLE EASY RECIPE, I KNOW, BUT I HAVEN'T SEEN IT PUBLISHED ANYWHERE, AND IT REALLY IS DELICIOUS. I HOPE YOU CAN USE IT.

SINCERELY,

Dave Ward

Dear Mr. Gardner,

    Just a note to thank you for your
recent letter.

    It is a pleasure to send you two
of my recipes. The ones I've enclosed
are favorites of both George's and mine.

    Best wishes,

        Warmly,

        Barbara Bush

VEGETABLE SALAD (SPINACH)
(serves 16)

2 lbs. freshly chopped spinach
      (You chop it!!)
10 hardboiled eggs, sliced
1 lb. bacon, cooked and crumbled
1 medium head of lettuce, shredded
1 cup sliced shallots
1 pkg. thawed frozen peas, uncooked

Place in order in layers in large salad bowl.

2 1/2 cups mayonnaise
2 1/2 cups sour cream
Salt and pepper
Worchestershire sauce to taste
Lemon juice to taste

Blend together and pour over peas.

1/2 cup grated swiss cheese

Add swiss cheese on top. Cover and chill 12
hours. Do <u>not</u> toss. Serve.

Barbara Bush

dallas cowboys football club

Roger Staubach's Spinach Salad

1 bag fresh spinach (wash, remove stems, tear in bite-size pieces)
4 ounces blue cheese - crumbled
1 can french fried onion rings

DRESSING:

1 can tomato soup	1/2 teaspoon salt
3/4 cup oil	1 teaspoon dry mustard
3/4 cup vinegar	1/4 teaspoon paprika
3/4 cup sugar	1 onion, quartered

In a tall bottle, mix dry ingredients first. Then add liquid ingredients, mixing well. Put onion in for flavor, but remove before serving. Makes enough dressing for two bags of spinach.

Dear Friend:

I'm pleased to share one of my very favorite recipes with you. This is a delicious recipe for luncheons and light suppers. Marianne and I enjoy it often, and our guests love it as well.

CHICKEN SALAD à la ROGERS

2 CUPS	Cooked chicken (white meat).
3	Dill pickles (non-kosher), skinned.
1/2 CUP	Chopped walnuts.
1/4 CUP	Slivered or chopped almonds.

Pick the chicken from the bone rather than cut it. Peel pickles with a potato peeler and chop. Mix all of the above ingredients lightly with mayonaise of choice. You may prefer to add chopped scallions. Season to taste and serve on a bed of crisp lettuce.

Happy eating!

FRL/sa

THE UNIVERSITY OF TEXAS SYSTEM

Office of the Chancellor

Dear Mr. Gardner:

Chancellor Walker has asked me to forward you his favorite salad recipe for inclusion in your Texas Sesquicentennial Cookbook. He also sends his best wishes for your endeavor.

Sincerely,

Sheila Simmons
Assistant to Chancellor

Enclosure

THE UNIVERSITY OF TEXAS SYSTEM

Office of the Chancellor

Twenty-Four Hour Salad

4 egg yolks
Juice of 1 lemon
1/4 cup cream
1/2 pint cream, whipped

1 pound seedless green grapes
1 cup shredded almonds
3 cups miniature marshmallows
2 cups pineapple chunks, drained

Cook the egg yolks, lemon juice and 1/4 cup of cream in a double boiler, stirring constantly, until thickened. Let the mixture set until it is cold. Add all remaining ingredients. Let stand for 24 hours after mixing.

Submitted by E. Don Walker, Chancellor
    The University of Texas System

CURRIED CHICKEN SALAD

2 cups cubed chicken
1 cup chopped celery
1 cup raisins
1 cup chopped apple
1 tablespoon grated onion

1 cup mayonnaise
½ teaspoon salt
½ teaspoon pepper
1 teaspoon curry powder

Mix all ingredients. Chill.

Mrs. Robert F. Jones (Annetta)

CHICKEN SALAD

1 chicken, cooked and chopped
½ pound seedless grapes
1 can water chestnuts, chopped
1 package toasted slivered almonds

1 cup chopped celery
1½ cups mayonnaise
1½ teaspoons curry powder
1½ teaspoons soy sauce

Combine ingredients and chill overnight. Serves 6 to 8.

Mrs. Lloyd Doggett (Libby)
Wife, State Senator

APRICOT GELATIN SALAD

2 (17½-ounce) cans apricot halves
3 packages apricot gelatin

2 cups sour cream
2 egg whites, whipped

Drain apricot halves, dissolve gelatin in heated juice. Put apricot halves in blender and blend until smooth. Add to gelatin when cool. Next, blend in sour cream. (Easiest way is to add a little gelatin mixture to sour cream and then blend all together.) Lastly, fold in whipped egg whites and pour into mold. Refrigerate several hours or overnight.

Mrs. Dan Goldsmith (Grace)

CHERRY COLA SALAD

1 (1-pound) can Bing cherries
1 (1-pound) can crushed pineapple
1 (6-ounce) package cherry or black cherry gelatin

1 (12-ounce) cola beverage
1 cup canned or packaged blanched slivered almonds
Sour cream, sweetened, to garnish

Drain cherries and pineapple, measure syrups, add water, if necessary to make 2 cups. Heat syrups to boiling, pour over gelatin, stir until gelatin is dissolved. Add cola beverage, chill until consistency of unbeaten egg white. Combine cherries, pineapple and almonds; fold in. Spoon into 8-cup mold. Chill until firm. Unmold. If desired, garnish with sour cream, sweetened to taste. Makes 10 to 12 servings.

Mrs. E. "Kika" de la Garza
Wife, U. S. Congressman

CRANBERRY SALAD

1 box orange gelatin
1 cup hot water
1 can whole cranberry sauce

1 large orange, peeled and cut into small pieces
½ cup pecans

Prepare gelatin with hot water and cranberry sauce; stir in orange pieces and pecans. Chill in individual molds or in pan to be cut into squares.

Mrs. Robert F. Jones (Annetta)

LEMON GELATIN SALAD

2 cups boiling water
1 cup Campbell's tomato soup
1 (8-ounce) package cream cheese, softened
2 packages lemon gelatin

2 cups chopped celery
½ cup chopped green pepper
½ cup grated onion
1 cup Miracle Whip salad dressing

Mix all ingredients. Refrigerate until set.

Mrs. O. M. Lynch (Annie)

ORANGE PINEAPPLE SALAD

1 (3-ounce) package orange gelatin
1 can mandarin oranges
1 can crushed pineapple, drained

1 (8-ounce) carton small curd cottage
  cheese
1 (8-ounce) container Cool Whip

Pour dry gelatin mix over fruit. Stir to melt. Add cottage cheese and Cool Whip. Fold into other mixture. Refrigerate. Keeps several days.

Mrs. Robert F. Jones (Annetta)

STRAWBERRY SALAD
Pretty and good! Great for taking!

1 (6-ounce) box strawberry gelatin
2 cups boiling water
1 package frozen strawberries, partially
  thawed

1 large can crushed pineapple
1 pint sour cream

Mix gelatin and water according to package directions. Add strawberries and pineapple, mixing well. Put half of mixture in dish, and refrigerate until firm. Spread sour cream over chilled gelatin, then put remaining gelatin mixture on top. Refrigerate until set.

Mrs. Floyd Kinser (Dorothy)

FROZEN WALDORF SALAD

2 eggs, lightly beaten
½ cup sugar
¼ cup pineapple juice
¼ cup lemon juice
⅛ teaspoon salt
Cornstarch (optional)

½ cup diced celery
½ cup drained crushed pineapple
2 medium apples, diced
½ cup broken English walnuts
1 cup whipping cream, whipped
Cherries, to garnish

Combine eggs, sugar, pineapple juice, lemon juice and salt. Cook until thick over low heat, stirring constantly. (You may add cornstarch, if necessary.) Cool. Important to cool. Add celery, pineapple, apples and nuts. Gently fold in whipped cream. Spoon into 8-inch square pan and freeze. To serve, cut into squares and garnish with cherries. Serves 8 to 10.

Paula Zahn
News Anchor
KRPC-TV
Houston, Texas
* Paula Zahn has moved to WNEV-TV, Boston

CABBAGE SLAW

1 head cabbage
1 green pepper
1 onion
1 cup sugar
1 cup vinegar

¾ cup salad oil
1 teaspoon salt
1 teaspoon mustard seed
1 teaspoon celery seed

Shred cabbage and divide in 2 parts. Chop green pepper and onion and divide. In large bowl, layer half the cabbage, green pepper and onion. Don't stir! Repeat with other half of cabbage, green pepper and onion. Sprinkle with sugar. Don't stir! In a separate bowl, mix vinegar, salad oil, salt, mustard and celery seed. Drizzle over top of vegetables. Don't stir! Cover tightly and let stand for 4 hours or overnight. Stir before serving. Note: This recipe is good for a crowd and can be made ahead as it keeps in refrigerator for several weeks if tightly covered.

Mrs. Tom Pollard (Carole)
Wife, Mayor of Kerrville, Texas

MOM'S POTATO SALAD

4 cups cooked, peeled, cubed potatoes
   (5 or 6 medium)
1 cup chopped hamburger dill pickle
   slices
½ cup chopped onion
2 eggs, hard-boiled and chopped

1 cup chopped green pepper
¼ teaspoon lemon pepper
1 teaspoon salt
1 tablespoon white vinegar
2 tablespoons vegetable oil
½ cup mayonnaise

Mix together well. Cover and chill. Makes about 5 cups.

Mrs. William R. Gardner (Mary Ann)

8 HOUR SALAD

1 medium head lettuce, shredded
1 cup chopped onion
1 cup chopped celery
1 cup chopped water chestnuts
½ teaspoon salt
1 cup grated mozzarella cheese
1 package frozen English peas, cooked
   and drained

2 cups Hellmann's mayonnaise
1 teaspoon sugar
¼ teaspoon pepper
½ cup Parmesan cheese
Parsley flakes
Bacon bits
Cherry tomatoes

Mix lettuce, onion, celery, water chestnuts, salt, mozzarella cheese, peas, mayonnaise, sugar, pepper and Parmesan cheese. Transfer to a large salad bowl or long pan. Top with parsley, bacon and cherry tomatoes. Note: I don't know where this salad gets its name, but you *do not* prepare it 8 hours before serving. It is best served the same day.

Mrs. Sam Jackson (Faye)

ORIENTAL SALAD

1 cup oil
⅓ cup sugar
⅓ cup catsup
½ teaspoon salt

⅓ cup vinegar
2 teaspoons Worcestershire sauce
1 small onion, chopped

Purée ingredients in blender or Cuisinart (using steel knife). Pour this dressing into an airtight container and store in refrigerator. Meanwhile put salad together.

SALAD
1 package fresh spinach
1 "big handful" fresh bean sprouts
1 can sliced water chestnuts
4 to 6 eggs, hard-boiled and sliced

1 cup sliced fresh mushrooms
4 to 6 bacon slices, cooked and
   crumbled

Mix all together and add dressing.

Mr. and Mrs. Norm Bulaich (Susie)
Former Professional Football Player

ASPARAGUS SALAD WITH SOY-LEMON DRESSING

1½ tablespoons vegetable oil
¼ teaspoon minced fresh or ½ teaspoon
  dried ginger
2 green onions, minced

½ cup chicken stock
1 tablespoon cider vinegar
1 teaspoon soy sauce
½ teaspoon sugar

Heat oil in small saucepan over medium-high heat. Add ginger and stir until beginning to color. Blend in minced onions and cook for 3 to 4 seconds. Mix in stock, vinegar, soy sauce and sugar. Set aside. (Dressing can be prepared 2 hours ahead to this point.)

SALAD

1 to 1¼ pounds thin asparagus stalks,
  cut diagonally into 1½ inch lengths
1 green onion, minced
1 head romaine lettuce, cut crosswise
  into ½-inch strips
¼ cup chopped salted cashews

1 pound fresh mushrooms, sliced
⅛ teaspoon or more freshly ground
  pepper
Salt, to taste
Fresh lemon juice, to taste

Pour water into steamer to within 1 inch of rack; set rack in place. Bring water to rapid boil over high heat. Steam asparagus until crisp-tender, about 5 minutes. Rinse under cold water to stop cooking process and set color. Drain and cool. Just before serving, place in large bowl the onion, lettuce, cashews, asparagus and mushrooms. Bring dressing to boil over medium-high heat. Let boil 30 seconds. Stir in the pepper. Taste and add salt, lemon juice and additional vinegar and pepper to attain tart, peppery flavor. Toss salad with simmering dressing and serve.

Mr. and Mrs. Dennis Swift (Mary)
Carshon's Deli

COBB SALAD

1 large head lettuce
Blue cheese, to taste
Vinaigrette dressing
1 large tomato
2 eggs, hard-boiled and chopped
1 large avocado

¼ cup chives
¼ cup chopped green onion
½ pound bacon, cooked crisp, drained
  and crumbled
1 large chicken breast, broiled and
  cubed

Finely chop lettuce. Mix with cheese and dressing. When ready to serve, add remaining ingredients. Mix gently. Add more dressing, as needed.

Delbert McClinton
Entertainer

MR. MAC'S SALAD DRESSING

2 cups safflower oil
1 cup fresh lemon juice
1 teaspoon packaged seasoned pepper
½ teaspoon salt
½ teaspoon dry mustard
1 teaspoon freshly ground pepper

⅛ teaspoon monosodium glutamate
1 tablespoon Worcestershire sauce
Dash Tabasco
¼ cup minced onion
1 egg, hard-boiled and minced

Put all ingredients in a blender or food processor. Process to blend. Refrigerate overnight to blend flavors. Serve over mixed salad greens or spinach and mushroom salad. Makes 3½ cups.

Willis C. McIntosh
The Carriage House
Fort Worth, Texas

HISTORIC DALLAS SALAD DRESSING AS CONCOCTED BY THE GREENE GROUP

1 or 2 fresh garlic cloves (or equivalent dried)
3 anchovy strips
1 cup oil (salad or olive)

½ cup vinegar (white or wine, not dark)
1 tablespoon Heinz chili sauce (*not* piquante: other seafood sauce may be used

Press garlic (be sure it is fresh and not dried out if using pods), mash anchovies with a fork, adding a fair amount of oil from the anchovy can. Put everything into a big wide-mouth Peter Pan peanut butter jar and shake until mixed, then let it all sit for several hours. Fish out the garlic pieces, if desired. Do not oversauce the salad. Extra anchovy strips may be used on individual salads. This amount should do quite a few servings.

A. C. Greene
Essayist

SPINACH SALAD DRESSING

½ cup sour cream
1 tablespoon salad dressing
½ teaspoon Beau Monde seasoning
1 teaspoon lemon juice

Pinch salt
1 tablespoon sweet milk
Ripe olives, to garnish

Blend all ingredients except olives. If desired, add olives for color.

Mrs. J. Herman Musick (Celeste)

ONION RELISH

½ gallon sliced onions
2 large cucumbers, sliced
2 small hot green peppers

¼ cup salt
1 cup ice water

Cover vegetables with salt and ice water. Let stand for 1 hour then drain well.

PASTE
3 cups vinegar
½ cup flour
2 tablespoons prepared mustard

1 teaspoon turmeric
1 cup sugar

Heat vinegar in large boiler. Make paste out of flour, mustard, turmeric and sugar. Add to boiling vinegar, stirring until smooth. Mix well-drained vegetables with hot paste and let mixture come to a slow boil. Seal in jars immediately.

Mrs. Maudi Walsh Roe

PEAR RELISH

8 large or 12 small pears (Keefer pears preferred)
3 medium onions
5 red bell peppers
3 green bell peppers
3 cups white vinegar

3 cups sugar
1 teaspoon celery seed
1 teaspoon white mustard seed
2 teaspoons salt
1 tablespoon cornstarch

Pare and core pears. Grind together with onions and peppers in food grinder. Drain off most of the juice. Mix vinegar, sugar, celery seed, mustard seed and salt. Pour over pear mixture and boil for 20 minutes. Add cornstarch mixed with a little water and boil for 15 more minutes. Pour into sterilized jars and seal. Makes 6 pints. Note: My wife, Beryl, and I make this together. I peel and grind. She measures and cooks. This is Beryl's father's recipe.

J. J. Pickle (Beryl)
U. S. Congressman

The "Cowboy" of Texas today has evolved from the durable Spanish vaquero who is his ancestor, but while this figure remains a worldwide symbol of what Texas and the American West has been and still is, Texas offers the finest in cultural events ranging from theatre, symphonies, and art to outstanding museums across the State. Yet despite the cultural diversity, it is still not too difficult to find a good rodeo almost anywhere in the Lone Star State.

KXAS-TV
Fort Worth/Dallas
an NBC affiliate

Dear Mr. Gardner,

I really am not much of a cook and therefore cannot do very much to contribute to your collection of recipes in your forthcoming book, However, I do have one thing that might be of interest to some people. Since I do have to watch my diet, I seem to have become somewhat of an authority on preparing low calorie omelettes. So, for whatever it may be worth here is a <u>Low Calorie Omelette</u>.

Using a commercial product, such as egg beaters, which are very low in cholestrol, the equivalent of two eggs, a little cold water, beaten to a frothy mess. Adding a little baking powder, about a teaspoonful, prepare chopped onion, pepper, green peppers, and tomatoes, if you like.

Saute these in a pan using a commercial product, such as Pam. While this is sauteing, spray Pam into an omelette pan. Put your beaten eggs into the omelette pan. Spread the sauted onions and peppers into the cooking omelette, and if you like, you can also add some Bacos and some diet cheese. When it's golden brown, put a little Mexican sauce, Ketchup, or whatever you like on omelettes, some toast, and you have a very filling low colorie, no cholestrol omelette.

I hope this helps some. Thank you for asking me to contribute and I look forward to seeing your book.

Sincerely,

Harold Taft

HT:pj

HAYNES & FULLENWEIDER
A PROFESSIONAL LEGAL CORPORATION

Dear Mr. Gardner:

Thank you for your letter of April 30, 1984. Mr. Haynes would be honored to have a couple of his favorite recipes included in a cookbook celebrating the Texas Sesquicentennial.

Attached are his recipes for Eggs Ranchero and Beef Stroganoff. Good luck with the cookbook and we look forward to seeing a copy.

Sincerely,

Judy Fogarty,
Assistant to Richard Haynes

/ju
Enc.

Eggs Ranchero

1 stick of butter or margarine
1 large white onion (finely chopped)
2 large fresh tomatoes (peeled and chopped)
4 green chili peppers (chopped)
1 dozen eggs

Melt butter in large frying pan, add onions, tomatoes and chili peppers. Cook over medium heat for about 30 minutes, stirring periodically to keep from sticking. In a large bowl, beat the eggs and pour into pan with tomato mixture. Stir until eggs are firm. Top with sliced jalapeno peppers. Serve with sausage and flour tortillas.

Richard "Racehorse" Haynes

DICK LOWE'S SUNRISE BREAKFAST

Fresh-squeezed orange juice poured over Blue Bell's Homemade Vanilla ice cream; 1 egg and 2 teaspoons honey mixed in blender, topped with 2 dashes nutmeg;
Scrambled eggs with butter and grated sharp Cheddar cheese;
Crisp bacon;
English muffins, butter and orange marmalade;
Coffee
Golf to follow

Dick Lowe
President, American Quasar Petroleum Company

CAPERED EGGS

12 eggs, hard-boiled
1 cup mayonnaise
1 cup sour cream
½ cup chives

½ cup capers
¼ cup pickle relish
1 teaspoon lemon pepper
½ teaspoon salt

Slice eggs in half lengthwise. Set aside. Prepare dressing by mixing remaining ingredients. In small casserole, layer egg halves and dressing, ending with dressing on top.

Mrs. C. Harold Brown (Carol)

CHILI SQUARES

8 eggs
½ cup flour
1 teaspoon baking powder

½ teaspoon salt
12 ounces Monterey Jack cheese, grated
2 (4-ounce) cans green chilies, chopped

Beat eggs until light. Blend flour with baking powder and salt and add to the eggs. Mix well. Fold in cheese and chilies and spread in greased 9x9x2-inch pan. Bake at 350° for 35 to 40 minutes. Cool for 5 minutes, then cut into small squares and use toothpicks to serve. A taste sensation, Texas style!

Ebby Halliday
Realtor

CHEESE AND GRITS CASSEROLE

6 cups boiling water
1½ cups grits
1 stick margarine (reserve a little to butter casserole)
1 pound Velveeta cheese, cut in pieces

1 teaspoon salt
1 teaspoon seasoned salt
Few dashes Tabasco sauce
3 eggs, well-beaten
Paprika, to taste

Boil water and grits in large pan until thick. Add margarine, cheese, salt, seasoned salt and Tabasco sauce. Fold in eggs. Transfer to large baking dish, sprinkle with paprika and bake at 250° for 1 hour.

Mrs. A. M. Pate, Jr.

CHEESE GRITS

¾ cup grits
3 cups boiling water
½ pound sharp Cheddar cheese

2 teaspoons seasoned salt
¾ stick butter
Dash Tabasco sauce

Stir grits into boiling water and cook 20 minutes. Add remaining ingredients. Transfer to baking dish and bake at 250° for 1 hour.

Mrs. Robert F. Jones (Annetta)

GRITS SOUFFLÉ

1½ cups hominy grits cereal
1½ teaspoons salt
6 cups boiling water
1½ sticks butter

1 pound Velveeta cheese
11 drops Tabasco sauce
4 eggs

Cook grits in salted water until thick, stirring constantly. While still hot, add butter and cheese, and stir until melted. Let cool. Mix in Tabasco sauce. Beat in eggs, 1 at a time. Bake in buttered 13x9-inch Pyrex pan at 350° for 45 minutes. Serves 12 to 15.

Mrs. Mark C. Hill (Kathy)

COWBOY QUICHE

5 cans whole green chilies
28 ounces Monterey Jack cheese, grated
5 eggs
1 can Pet evaporated milk

2 tablespoons flour
Salt, to taste
Pepper, to taste

Layer 2½ cans split chilies on the bottom of a 13x9-inch baking pan. Sprinkle half of the cheese over the chilies. Top with remaining chilies and another layer of cheese. Beat eggs with milk, flour, salt and pepper. Pour egg mixture over chili-cheese layers. Bake at 350° for 20 to 30 minutes. Let sit for 10 minutes before cutting.

Mrs. James A. Baker, III
Wife, White House Chief of Staff

LARRY HAGMAN'S COUNTRY QUICHE

1 (2-pound) bag frozen French fries
1 large yellow onion, finely chopped
½ pound butter
1 box frozen mustard greens
1 dozen eggs

1 pint heavy cream
1 pound leftover cheese
Salt, to taste
Pepper, to taste
Nutmeg, to taste

Sauté frozen French fries and onion in butter until light brown, turning frequently. Grease a large Pyrex, copper or ovenproof dish. Parboil mustard greens and drain. Set aside. Beat eggs and cream as if for omelet, and set aside. Grate cheese. Layer half the potatoes and onion in pan, add all of the mustard greens, half the cheese and season with salt, pepper and nutmeg. Then pour a little of the egg and cream mixture over top. For second layer: add rest of potatoes and onion, then cheese and pour remainder of egg and cream mixture over top. Gently pierce through layers with fork so egg mixture will soak in. Bake at 350° for 1 hour. Serve alone, with salad or baked ham. You can also dice the ham, leftover steak or chicken and put into the casserole. The *nutmeg* is *very* important.

Larry Hagman
Actor

DELICIOUS BRUNCH QUICHE

6 eggs
2 zucchini or broccoli
¼ cup milk
1½ cups grated cheese (Swiss and sharp Cheddar)

8 mushrooms, sliced
3 tablespoons whole wheat flour
1 frozen deep dish pie crust
Ripe olives (optional)

Beat eggs. Add zucchini or broccoli, milk, cheese, mushrooms and flour, 1 at a time, stirring to mix. Pour into pie crust. Decorate top with zucchini slices and cheese. Sprinkle on olives, if desired. Bake at 350° for 45 minutes or until firm.

Linda Schaefer
KTBC-TV
Austin, Texas

SPINACH QUICHE
Without a crust.

1 pound small curd cottage cheese
½ package frozen chopped spinach, thawed and drained
3 eggs, beaten

¼ cup butter, melted
3 tablespoons flour
6 ounces Cheddar cheese, grated

Mix ingredients and transfer to a shallow casserole or quiche pan. Bake at 350° for 1 hour. Let stand for 10 minutes before cutting. Note: This can be used as an hors d'oeuvre, as a main course for lunch or as a vegetable complement to roast or steak. Serves 6 to 8.

Mrs. Ardell M. Young (Marjorie)

SPINACH SOUFFLÉ

1½ cups milk
½ cup dry skimmed milk
1½ teaspoons salt
1 teaspoon white pepper
4 eggs, separated
¼ teaspoon basil

1½ cups grated sharp Cheddar cheese
Fresh chopped parsley
1 teaspoon Worcestershire sauce
2 or more cups chopped uncooked spinach
1 onion, chopped

Heat 1 cup milk to simmering. Beat together remaining milk, dry milk, salt and pepper. Add to hot milk and simmer for 5 minutes, stirring constantly. Let cook a little and add the egg yolks, basil, cheese and chopped parsley. Add Worcestershire sauce and stir well. Add spinach and onion. Fold in stiffly beaten egg whites and pour into oiled casserole dish. Bake at 300° for approximately 45 minutes.

Shane D. Moon
Kay Bearden
Trinity Terrace

MANICOTTI "MAESTRO"

8 manicotti shells
2 teaspoons olive oil
6 cups fresh spinach, washed and stems
   removed
2 cups ricotta cheese
Oregano leaves

Salt, to taste
Pepper, to taste
2 cups béchamel sauce
1 ripe avocado
1 cup Italian tomato sauce
2 ounces grated Parmesan cheese

Cook the manicotti shells in plenty of boiling salted water until done but firm (al dente). In a skillet, heat the olive oil and quickly sauté the spinach. Take off the fire and drain well. Let them cool off and mix with the cheese, a pinch of oregano and salt and pepper. Fill the cooked shells with the cheese mixture and place in a buttered casserole about ¼ inch apart, cover with béchamel sauce, 2 thin slices of avocado on top of each shell and top with a teaspoon of tomato sauce. Sprinkle with Parmesan cheese and bake at 300° for 25 minutes. Makes 4 servings of 2.

Vito Ciraci
The Fort Worth Club

PRESIDENT REAGAN'S FAVORITE MACARONI AND CHEESE

½ pound macaroni
1 teaspoon butter
1 egg, beaten
1 teaspoon salt

1 teaspoon dry mustard
1 tablespoon hot water
1 cup milk
3 cups grated sharp cheese

Boil macaroni in water until tender and drain thoroughly. Stir in butter and egg. Mix salt and mustard with hot water and add to milk. Add cheese, leaving enough to sprinkle on top. Pour into buttered casserole, add milk, sprinkle with cheese. Bake at 350° for about 45 minutes or until custard is set and top is crusty.

Ronald Reagan
President
The United States of America

The "Shrine of Texas Liberty," Mission San Antonio de Valero-The Alamo- is a widely recognized symbol of Texas for both natives and non-natives of the Lone Star State. The familiar chapel was constructed in 1754, and it and its walled bastions served as the final battleground for approximately 178 Texans who sought to hold off the vastly superior Mexican army. The battle has provided a group of martyrs around whose memory Texans then and now have rallied. There are plans to renovate Alamo Plaza for the 1986 Texas Sesquicentennial celebration.

CITY OF SAN ANTONIO

SAN ANTONIO, TEXAS

HENRY G. CISNEROS
MAYOR

Pepper Steak

1 1/2 pounds round steak, cut in strips
1 tablespoon paprika
2 garlic cloves, pressed
2 tablespoons margarine
1 cup onion slices
2 green peppers, cut in strips
2 large fresh tomatoes, cut in 8 pieces each
1 cup beef broth or 1 bouillon cube dissolved in 1 cup water
1/4 cup water
2 tablespoons cornstarch
2 tablespoons soy sauce
3 cups hot cooked rice

Sprinkle steak with paprika and allow to stand while preparing
other ingredients. Cook steak and garlic in margarine until
meat is browned. Add onions and green peppers; continue
cooking until vegetables are wilted. Add tomatoes and broth,
cover and simmer for about 15 minutes. Blend water with
cornstarch and soy sauce. Stir into steak and cook until
thickened. Serve over fluffy rice.

Henry G. Cisneros

MARCUS

DEAR MR. GARDNER:

The attached is one of my very favorite recipes
and was taken from "Helen Corbitt Cooks for
Company" by Helen Corbitt.

Sincerely,

Stanley Marcus

Stanley Marcus

SM:wl
Enclosure

MARCUS

BOILED BEEF BRISKET
(For 10 to 12)

1 5- to 6-pound piece of brisket
1 large onion stuck with 2 cloves
1 bay leaf
1 piece celery with leaves
2 carrots
Few springs of parsley
6 peppercorns
1 bottle beer (you may omit)
1 tablespoon salt

Place the beef in a kettle and cover with boiling water.
Add rest of ingredients. Bring to a boil; reduce the
heat to simmer, and cook for 3 to 4 hours or until
meat is tender. Add 1 tablespoon salt after 1 hour's
cooking. Do not overcook or meat will be stringy and
will not slice properly. Remove, and keep warm. Cut
off any excess fat before serving, but leave on while
cooking. If you wish brisket for an entrée, strain the
juices left from cooking, skim off the fat, and for each
cup of liquid, add:

1 cup whipping cream
¼ cup grated horseradish or
　horseradish sauce
1 teaspoon chopped chives
½ teaspoon dry mustard
¼ cup diced apple

Cook until reduced to a thin sauce. Serve over thinly
sliced meat.

FROM HELEN CORBITT COOKS FOR COMPANY BY HELEN CORBITT.
COPYRIGHT 1974 BY HELEN CORBITT.
REPRINTED BY PERMISSION OF HOUGHTON-MIFFLIN COMPANY.

Roy Rogers — Dale Evans Museum

15650 Seneca Road, Victorville, California 92392

Roy Rogers   Dale Evans Rogers

CHILI TEX--

1 Can Chili with beans   Chopped onions
1 Can White or yellow hominy   Grated cheese

In a baking dish, arrange in alternate layers: chili,
cheese, onions and hominy. Top with grated cheese and
bake until onions are tender and cheese is thoroughly melted.
Bake in a moderate oven of 350 degrees.

Dale Evans Rogers

Dan Rather's Favorite Brisket

Brisket
Celery salt
Garlic salt
Lemon pepper
Onion salt
3 ounces Liquid Smoke
Salt
Pepper
1/2 cup Worcestershire sauce
1 small bottle barbecue sauce

Sprinkle brisket with celery salt, garlic salt, lemon pepper
and onion salt. Center in a heavy piece of foil, sprinkle with
Liquid Smoke, and fold sides of foil over to seal in packet.
Refrigerate overnight. Six and a half hours before serving:
open packet, season with salt, pepper and Worcestershire
sauce, reseal and cook in a slow oven (300 degrees) for
5 hours. Uncover and pour barbecue sauce over brisket.
Cook 1 additional hour, uncovered. Let sit for 20 minutes
before slicing. Serve with remaining sauce.

Dan Rather

LON EVANS
SHERIFF

Dear Mr. Farkas:

I wish to thank you for including my Jailhouse Chili recipe in your collection. The recipe is as follows:

SHERIFF LON EVANS' FAMOUS JAILHOUSE CHILI RECIPE

1/8 lb suet finely chopped	1 tablespoon salt
3 lbs round steak or chuck, coarsely ground	1 teaspoon red pepper
	2 cloves garlic, minced
6 tablespoons chili powder	1-1/2 quarts water
1 tablespoon ground Oregano	1 teaspoon Tabasco
1 tablespoon crushed Cumin seed	3 tablespoons Masa meal
	1 8-oz can tomato sauce

In Dutch oven, fry suet until crisp; add ground meat and brown; add seasonings and water; heat to boil. Reduce heat, cover and simmer for 1-1/2 hours. Skim off fat if desired. Stir in Masa meal and simmer, uncovered, for 30 min. Stir occasionally. Very good mixed with pinto beans.

Sincerely,

LON EVANS, Sheriff
Tarrant County, Texas

LE:jl

Bob Lilly's Favorite Dish: Beef Stew

Ingredients:

    ½ to 1 lb. stew meat
    1 tsp. Beef Bouillon granules
    12-oz. can tomato juice
    2 16-oz. cans tomatoes, chopped
    2/3 of an onion, chopped
    2 stalks celery, sliced
    1 bay leaf
    2 small potatoes, diced
    2 carrots, diced
    1/3 cup peas
    1/3 cup corn
    salt, pepper
    water, as needed

Directions:

   Boil the stew meat with the beef bouillon
granules in 4 cups water for 2 to 4 hours.
Optional: refrigerate until cool, then take
fat layer off. Add vegetables and seasonings;
simmer 2-3 hours. Add water as needed.

Bob Lilly

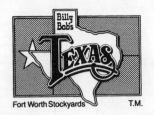

BILLY BOB BARNETT's
WORLD'S LARGEST HONKY-TONK
TEXAS STYLE CHILI

10 lb. Chili ground meat

1 Cup Chili Powder (hot)

1 Cup Chili Powder (mild)

3/4 Cup Paprika

1/2 Cup Cumino (cumin)

1/4 Cup Garlic Powder

1/4 Cup Salt

1/8 Cup Crushed Red Chili (Jap Chili)

1 lb. Suet

3 Qts. Water

1/4 Cup Sugar (twenty min. before pulling)

Add fat first, then meat and seasoning to fat.

Add water after cooks two hours.

Cook 3 hours total

Stir Occasionally

Billy Bob Barnett

SOUTHWEST ATHLETIC CONFERENCE

UNIVERSITY OF ARKANS
BAYLOR UNIVERS
UNIVERSITY OF HOUST
RICE UNIVERS
SOUTHERN METHODIST UNIVERS
THE UNIVERSITY OF TEXAS AT AUS
TEXAS A&M UNIVERS
TEXAS CHRISTIAN UNIVERS
TEXAS TECH UNIVERS

This is one of my favorite recipes:

GOLDEN LASAGNE
(Basic recipe makes 8 servings)

3 tablespoons butter or regular margarine
½ pound fresh mushrooms, sliced
½ cup finely chopped onion
½ cup chopped green pepper
1 10 3/4-once can condensed cream of chicken soup
1/3 cup milk
¼ cup chopped pimientos
½ teaspoon dried basil leaves
8 lasagne noodles (8 onces), cooked and drained
1 16-ounce carton creamed small-curd cottage cheese (about 1½ cups)
3 cups cubed cooked chicken
2 cups shredded Cheddar cheese
½ cup grated Parmesan cheese

OVEN: 25 minutes cooking time

Melt butter in 2-quart saucepan over medium heat, about 2 minutes.
Add mushrooms, onion and green pepper and saute 5 minutes or until
tender. Remove from heat. Stir in chicken soup, milk, pimientos and
basil. Arrange 4 noodles in greased 13x9x2-inch (3-quart) glass
baking dish. Top with layers of: ½ of the sauce, ½ of the cottage
cheese, ½ of the chicken, ½ of the Cheddar cheese, and ½ of the
Parmesan cheese. Add 4 more noodles and remaining ingredients in
layers. Cook in 400° oven 25 minutes or until bubbly. Let stand
10 minutes. Serve.

Best regards,

Fred Jacoby
Commissioner

The Senate of
The State of Texas
Austin 78711

CHET EDWARDS
STATE SENATOR
DISTRICT 9

Committees:

STATE AFFAIRS
EDUCATION
HEALTH AND HUMAN
RESOURCES
Vice Chairman,
SUBCOMMITTEE ON
CONSUMER AFFAIRS

Dear Russell:

As a life long bachelor, my favorite recipe is:

STOUFFER'S BEEF TERIYAKI

Directions: pull frozen plastic bag out of box, place in boiling water for 15 minutes and eat.
For servings of 2, pull out 2 bags and boil for 15 minutes, preferably add candlelight.

Sincerely,

Chet Edwards
State Senator

CE:sa

GENTLING

Dear Chris,

This is my recipe which I invented to honor the great composer George Frideric Handel. It is easy to prepare, and I hope that your readers enjoy it.

FILET OF BEEF G.F. HANDEL
(servings for four)

Ingredients

4 med. size bacon-wrapped beef filets
4 slices of good rye bread
4 slices of pate de fois gras 1/4" thick
clarified butter
McCormick's beef gravy mix — I pkg.
I can large whole button mushrooms
I can beef stock
Madeira Wine

Seasonings

garlic powder
tarragon
basil
fresh ground black pepper
Worchestershire sauce
chopped parsley

Procedure

I. MADEIRA SAUCE

Make the sauce according to package directions — using beef stock, a little of the mushroom liquid, and the Madeira instead of water. Season the sauce with the following:

    1/4 tsp. garlic powder or to taste
    1/2 tsp. tarragon (dried)
    1/4 tsp. basil (dried)
    pepper to taste
    butter bits for enrichment
This sauce should taste distinctly of Madeira

(over)

II. THE FILETS

Season both sides of each filet with the following: garlic powder, a pinch of both tarragon and basil, Worchestershire sauce
and black pepper.

In a small amount of clarified butter pan fry the filets until
very brown on one side, then turn them, then cook briefly or to
desired doneness.

III. THE CROUTONS

With a drinking glass or cookie cutter cut out 4 circles of Rye
bread the size of the filets and fry them in butter until crisp.

IV. To assemble

Put a generous layer of pate on the rye croutons and place each
on a plate. Place the filet on each crouton and put one of the
large cooked mushrooms on top of the filet. These mushrooms have
been cooked in the sauce. Pour the sauce artfully on the filet
in a cross pattern, sprinkle it with a little parsley and serve.

Serve with buttered asperagus

For a wine I recommend a Chateau Lafitte Rothschild 1959 in com-
memoration of the Bicentennial of Handel's death, but for some of
us a cold German or Dutch beer will be quite sufficient.

P.S. Chris, our book, OF BIRDS AND TEXAS, is about to go to press,
     and your copy should be ready for delivery next March.

                                         Best wishes,

                                         Stuart Gentling

Lucifer Hummingbird
SWG.

Harold Patterson
Mayor

FAVORITE RECIPE OF
MAYOR HAROLD PATTERSON
CITY OF ARLINGTON

PATTERSON'S CHILI

4 lbs. coarse ground beef
6 tablespoons chili blend powder
1 teaspoon ground oregano
1 teaspoon ground comino
1 teaspoon paprika
1 tablespoon salt
4 cans tomato sauce
Paste (1 tablespoon flour and one-half cup water)

Mix the chili powder, oregano, comino, paprika and salt, then set aside.
In a large skillet place the ground beef. Cook slowly until all meat
has turned light brown color. Stir 3 or 4 times. Add 4 cans tomato
sauce and dry ingredients. Simmer one hour. Let cool. After it has
cooled you may add a mixture of flour and water paste.
Reheat until it thickens.

*Note: Coarsley ground venison meat works great.

Texas

House of Representatives

Dear Mr. Gardner:

I have enclosed a poem for your cookbook.

TRAVELS WITH CHARLIE

Get in car

Back out of drive

Observe all regulations of the road

Turn in to closest McDonalds

Order two cheeseburgers, small fries,

Medium Dr. Pepper

Pay, Eat, Enjoy

Sincerely,

Charles Gandy

CG/jw

VEAL MEDALLIONS WITH SHRIMP AND LUMP CRAB MEAT

12 (2-ounce) loin or tenderloin veal medallions
Flour
Salt
White pepper
2 sticks butter
1 shallot, chopped

Chablis (for deglazing)
1½ cups heavy cream
12 large shrimp, peeled and deveined
8 ounces fresh lump crab meat
1 tablespoon chopped parsley

Season medallions with flour, salt and pepper. Melt 1 stick butter in a heavy skillet; sauté the veal medallions for about 2 minutes, add shallot and sauté for 1 more minute or until shallot pieces are transparent and glossy looking. Deglaze with chablis, remove veal from skillet, pour 1 cup cream in skillet and reduce. In a separate skillet, melt the remaining butter and sauté the shrimp and crab meat. Place medallions on platter, top with shrimp and crab meat, set aside and keep warm. Take the cream and shallot reduction and combine with the juice from the crab meat and shrimp plus the remaining cream. Season to taste with salt, ground white pepper and chopped parsley. Let simmer for a few minutes to blend the veal and seafood tastes. Pour over the veal, shrimp and crab meat. Serve at once. Accompany with fettuccine and asparagus spears.

Dallas Country Club

BEEF STROGANOFF

1½ pounds top sirloin beef
1 large onion
½ pound fresh mushrooms
Butter
½ cup sherry

¼ cup water
Salt, to taste
Pepper, to taste
½ pint sour cream

Cut meat into 1-inch cubes. Sauté meat, onion and mushrooms in butter until brown. Add the sherry, water, salt and pepper. Simmer for 5 minutes, then turn off fire. Stir in the sour cream and serve immediately over hot buttered egg noodles.

Richard "Racehorse" Haynes
Attorney at Law

SOUTHERN STEAK BAR-BE-QUE

¼ cup butter, softened
2 tablespoons dry mustard
2 teaspoons salt
2 teaspoons sugar

¾ teaspoon paprika
¼ teaspoon pepper
1 (2-pound) sirloin steak

For seasoned butter, blend butter, mustard, salt, sugar, paprika and pepper. Spread half of this butter on 1 side of the steak. Brown steak, buttered side down. As it browns, spread remaining mixture on top side of steak. Turn and brown this side, too. Remove steak to broiler.

BROILING SAUCE
¼ cup olive oil
2 tablespoons Worcestershire sauce
2 tablespoons catsup

¾ teaspoon sugar
¾ teaspoon salt

Mix ingredients. Add skillet drippings to the sauce and brush on steak. Broil for 5 to 7 minutes on each side, basting frequently with sauce.

Mr. and Mrs. Norm Bulaich (Susie)
Former Professional Football Player

CHICKEN FRIED STEAK

2 pounds inside round steak (at least ½ inch thick)
Flour

Batter
Peanut oil

Tenderize both sides of meat with mallet and cut away any gristle or fat. Cut this into pieces no larger than 6 inches in diameter. Completely flour each piece. Dip into batter and drain, then flour again, shaking off excess. Deep fry in peanut oil (or any high grade vegetable oil), preheated to 325° to 350°. Cook approximately 6 to 8 minutes or until golden brown.

BATTER
3 tablespoons sugar
½ teaspoon Tony Chachere's creole seasoning (seasoning spices at grocery)

1 egg
1 tablespoon baking powder
2 cups milk

Stir all ingredients with about half the milk until smooth. Then add remaining milk and stir again.

Mr. and Mrs. Sam Gann (Libby)

BRANDYWINE BEEF

3 pounds boneless chuck or other beef
   suitable for potting
Salt
Freshly ground pepper
⅛ teaspoon cinnamon
2 tablespoons cooking oil

1 small onion, sliced
1 garlic clove (optional)
3 tablespoons brandy (or bourbon)
1 bay leaf
½ cup dry white wine

Sprinkle meat with salt, pepper and cinnamon. Be meager with cinnamon! Heat oil in a large pot over a medium high heat, until hot but not smoking. Add meat and brown it well on all sides. Add the onion slices and let them brown. Add garlic, if desired. Reduce heat. Heat brandy, ignite and pour over meat. Spoon the burning brandy over the meat until the flame dies. Add the bay leaf and wine, cover tightly, reduce heat, and cook about 1½ hours, or until meat is fork-tender but not too soft. It should retain a little firmness. After first hour of cooking, turn the meat over, and taste gravy to adjust seasonings. When meat is done, remove it to a hot platter. Remove bay leaf, increase heat under liquid and boil rapidly until reduced by a third. To serve, cut meat into ½-inch slices and pour gravy over it.

Mrs. James C. Wright, Jr. (Betty)
Wife, U. S. Congressman

BEEF BURGUNDY

½ pound salt pork, diced
2 dozen small white onions
4 pounds lean chuck beef, cut into 2-
   inch cubes
Salt, to taste
Pepper, to taste
2 garlic cloves
2 bay leaves

1 piece orange peel
1 teaspoon thyme
4 large parsley sprigs
½ teaspoon grated nutmeg
½ teaspoon marjoram
1 bottle red Burgundy wine
2 dozen mushrooms

Brown pork until crisp. Remove pork and brown onions. Remove onions and brown beef. Return pork to pan and add salt, pepper, garlic, bay leaves, orange peel, thyme, parsley, nutmeg and marjoram. Barely cover with wine. Cover tightly and cook on low heat for 2 hours and 45 minutes. Add onions and mushrooms and cook 15 more minutes. Serve with French bread. Serves 8 to 10 people.

Mrs. G. E. Lehmann (Frances)
Real Estate/Investments

SEASONED STEAK WITH MUSHROOM GRAVY

Seasoning mix
1 (2-pound) steak
Flour
2 tablespoons oil

2½ cups water
1 cup sliced fresh mushroom
1 small onion, sliced (optional)
1/4 cup sliced sweet pepper (optional)

Sprinkle 1 teaspoon seasoning mix on each side of steak. Dredge with flour. Heat oil in a heavy skillet with a tight fitting lid, and brown steak on both sides. Add water and cook over low heat for about 1½ hours. Add mushrooms the last 15 minutes. If desired, onion and sweet pepper may be added with the mushrooms. Remove steak, and if needed, thicken gravy with flour and water mixture. Serve over rice or creamed potatoes. For seasoning mix, mix spices and store in tightly covered container. May be used with beef, poultry, salad and vegetables.

SEASONING MIX
1 tablespoon salt
1 tablespoon black pepper
1 tablespoon celery salt
1 tablespoon parsley flakes
1 tablespoon monosodium glutamate

1 teaspoon oregano
1 tablespoon ground sage
1 teaspoon thyme
1 tablespoon garlic salt
1 teaspoon onion powder

Mr. and Mrs. Jack Bryant (Clarise)
Artist and Sculptor

THREE DAY BRISKET

1 brisket
2 tablespoons Liquid Smoke
1 tablespoon salt

1 tablespoon onion salt
1 tablespoon garlic salt

First day: baste unbaked brisket with Liquid Smoke and salt. Wrap in foil and refrigerate for 24 hours. Second day: rub brisket with onion salt and garlic salt. Rewrap in foil and bake at 300° for 5 hours. Return to refrigerator overnight. Third day: slice cold brisket and cover with the following sauce. Rewrap in foil and bake at 350° for 1 hour. For sauce, combine all ingredients in saucepan. Cook until well blended, then pour over brisket.

SAUCE
1½ tablespoons brown sugar
½ cup catsup
¼ cup water
1 tablespoon celery salt
1 teaspoon salt
3 tablespoons butter

½ teaspoon dry mustard
2 tablespoons Lea & Perrins
  Worcestershire sauce
Dash pepper
1 tablespoon Liquid Smoke

Mrs. Stuart Schuster

SPACEY SPAGHETTI SAUCE

2 large cans whole tomatoes
3 small cans tomato paste
3 large cans tomato sauce
½ teaspoon soda (to remove acid)
¼ cup olive oil
3 onions, finely chopped
11 large garlic cloves, finely chopped
2 to 3 green peppers, chopped
2 pork ribs, wrapped in cheesecloth bag
 for easy removal
2 beef ribs, wrapped in cheesecloth bag
 for easy removal

2 teaspoons Italian herb seasoning
2 teaspoons sweet basil
1 teaspoon thyme
2 teaspoons oregano
⅓ bunch fresh parsley, chopped
2 bay leaves
3 teaspoons black pepper
3 teaspoons salt
4 teaspoons sugar
½ cup freshly grated Romano or
 Parmesan cheese

Into a large crockpot (you really can make it better this way), pour tomatoes, paste and sauce. Add soda and stir well. In a frying pan, add olive oil, onions, garlic, green peppers and meat. When all these are slightly browned, pour contents into crockpot. Cover, place on low setting, and simmer for 6 to 8 hours. Add water as needed. After 6 to 8 hours, remove the meat, add herbs, seasonings, sugar and cheese. Cover and continue to simmer on low setting until sauce reaches desired consistency.

Alan L. Bean
Astronaut

MORE
A one-dish dinner.

2 onions, diced
1 green pepper, diced
1 can mushrooms, diced
2 small garlic cloves, diced
Salad oil
1½ pounds ground round beef
1 tablespoon chili powder
Salt

Pepper
1 can tomatoes
1 can tomato sauce
1 package frozen English peas
1 can whole kernel corn
1½ cups cooked shell macaroni
Sharp Cheddar cheese, grated

Sauté onions, green pepper, mushrooms and garlic in a small amount of salad oil; add ground meat and chili powder. Salt and pepper to taste. Add tomatoes and tomato sauce and let simmer for awhile. Then add peas, corn and cooked macaroni. Pour into a large Pyrex dish and sprinkle with sharp Cheddar cheese. Bake at 350° for 30 minutes.

Mrs. W. P. Clements, Jr. (Rita C.)
Wife, Governor of Texas
1978-1982

TALAGARINI

8 ounces noodles
2 tablespoons fat
2 cups chopped onion
1 teaspoon chopped garlic or ½ teaspoon
    garlic powder
1 green pepper, chopped

2 small cans tomato sauce
2 pounds ground steak
2 teaspoons salt
½ teaspoon black pepper
3 tablespoons Morton's chili blend
1 pound American cheese, grated

Boil noodles in salted water until tender; drain and set aside. Simmer fat, onion, garlic and pepper. Stir in tomato sauce and continue to simmer slowly for 10 to 15 minutes. Brown ground steak, add 2 teaspoons salt, the black pepper and chili blend. Mix with tomato sauce mixture. Combine with noodles and grated cheese, mixing well. Bake in a moderate oven for 30 minutes, or freeze for later use. Yields 2 casseroles (1 gallon.)

Jane Keel
Vice President
Central Bank and Trust

TONY & JACLYN'S LONDON CHILI

1 pound pinto beans
2 pounds sirloin steak
2 pounds lean ground steak
¾ cup oil, divided
2 green peppers
2 medium onions
7 garlic cloves
4 teaspoons chili powder

3 teaspoons cumin
¼ teaspoon cayenne pepper
2 chili peppers
1 (6-ounce) can tomato paste
2 (10-ounce) cans tomatoes
Salt, to taste
Pepper, to taste

Wash beans and cook for about 45 minutes or until tender. Set aside. Cut sirloin into ¾-inch cubes and brown with ground steak and ½ cup oil in a large pot. Drain well. Chop green peppers and onions well. (Process in blender until it's a slush.) In large pan with rest of oil, cook these for about 5 minutes. Pour into meat. Press garlic and put in chili powder, cumin, cayenne pepper and well-chopped chili peppers. Add tomato paste. Crush canned tomatoes with a fork and stir into chili. Simmer about 45 minutes. Stir in beans and simmer for about 5 minutes. Season with salt and pepper. If you want to curl your toes, add more cayenne pepper. But be careful.

Mr. and Mrs. Tony Richmond (Jaclyn Smith)

CHILI RECIPE OF SENATOR JOHN TOWER OF TEXAS

3 pounds chili meat
2 large onions, finely chopped
1 (15-ounce) can tomato sauce
1 cup water
1 teaspoon Tabasco sauce
4 heaping tablespoons chili powder
1 heaping tablespoon oregano
1 teaspoon comino (cumin)
1 garlic clove, pressed

1 teaspoon salt
Black pepper, to taste (optional)
1 teaspoon cayenne pepper
1 level teaspoon paprika
1 dozen red peppers, chopped
4 to 5 serrano chili peppers, chopped
2 tablespoons flour
Water

Sear meat and onions until meat is gray. Add tomato sauce and 1 cup water to searing meat and onion mixture. Add Tabasco sauce, chili powder, oregano, comino, garlic, salt, pepper, cayenne pepper, paprika, red peppers and serrano chili peppers. (Scrape seeds from peppers to reduce hot taste.) Simmer for 1 hour and 15 minutes. Make a thickening by mixing flour and water, and add to chili. Simmer an additional 30 minutes.

Hon. John Tower
United States Senate

SUE'S CHILI

1 large onion, chopped
3 pounds ground meat (2 pounds ground venison or lean beef with 1 pound hamburger)
½ tablespoon or more salt
2 teaspoons garlic powder
1 tablespoon ground comino
1 teaspoon paprika

⅓ cup chili powder
1 (14½-ounce) can canned tomatoes, mashed
2 (8-ounce) cans tomato sauce
2 (8-ounce) cans water
¼ cup masa harina or flour (for thickening)

Brown onion and ground meat. Add salt, garlic powder, comino, paprika and chili powder. Stir well. Add canned tomatoes, tomato sauce and water. Stir well. Cover partially and simmer over very low heat for 1 hour. Add more water, if needed. Mix the masa harina or flour with 1 cup or more of warm water. Stir until smooth, then add to the chili. Simmer for 30 minutes. Yields about 2 quarts.

Mrs. William D. Balthrope (Sue)
Wife, Mayor of Alamo Heights, Texas

HEARTY MEAL IN A SKILLET

1 pound ground meat
1½ cups chopped onion
½ cup chopped green pepper
1 small can tomato sauce
4 tablespoons catsup
2 to 3 tablespoons chili powder
½ teaspoon salt
¼ teaspoon pepper

1 (10-ounce) package frozen whole
   kernel corn
1½ cups grated Cheddar or longhorn
   cheese
1½ cups biscuit mix
1 cup milk
2 eggs

Preheat oven to 350°. Brown meat, onion and green pepper. Add tomato sauce, catsup, chili powder, salt and pepper. Mix well and add corn. Pour into 9-inch ovenproof skillet and distribute evenly. Sprinkle with cheese. Prepare biscuit mix with mixture of milk and eggs, beating until smooth. Pour over meat mixture. Bake for 30 minutes or until a toothpick inserted in center comes out clean. Let stand at least 5 minutes before serving. Serve with a green salad. Serves 4.

Mike Millsap
State Representative

LASAGNA I

2 pounds ground round
3 garlic cloves
1 medium onion
2 tablespoons olive oil
2 teaspoons oregano
2 teaspoons salt
1 teaspoon pepper
1 tablespoon grated Parmesan cheese
1 tablespoon grated Romano cheese

3 (12-ounce) cans tomato paste
2 (15-ounce) cans tomato sauce
1 (12-ounce) can water
1 (8-ounce) package lasagna noodles
3 or 4 packages mozzarella cheese
   (sliced or grated)
1 (12-ounce) carton cottage cheese
Grated Parmesan cheese

Brown the meat, garlic and onion in the olive oil. Add the oregano, salt, pepper, Parmesan cheese and Romano cheese. Mix in the tomato paste, tomato sauce and water. Simmer in a large pot for 1½ hours. Cook lasagna according to package directions; drain. In the lasagna baking dish, layer the ingredients beginning with the meat sauce. Cover that with a layer of lasagna noodles, then mozzarella cheese. Spoon some cottage cheese over the mozzarella. Continue to layer the ingredients, ending with the meat sauce. Sprinkle Parmesan cheese over the top. Cover with foil and bake at 350° for 30 minutes.

John V. McMillan
Coors Distributing Company

LASAGNA II

2 pounds hamburger meat
Garlic cloves, chopped (to taste)
Vegetable oil
Oregano
Salt
Pepper

1 can tomato sauce
1 can peeled tomatoes
1 (12-ounce) package lasagna noodles
1 package sliced Swiss cheese
1 large carton cottage cheese
Grated Parmesan cheese

Brown meat and garlic in vegetable oil. Add oregano, salt, pepper, tomato sauce and peeled tomatoes. Simmer for 20 to 30 minutes. Boil noodles according to package directions. Lightly grease a glass casserole dish. When noodles are done, drain and place 1 layer of noodles, half the Swiss cheese, half the cottage cheese and half the meat mixture. Sprinkle with Parmesan. Repeat. Bake at 350° for 30 minutes. Can easily be made ahead. Serves 6.

Norma Lea Beasley

MEAT CONCERN

1 large can cream-style corn
1 large can tomatoes
Salt
3 tablespoons butter
1 package fine noodles
¼ cup chopped onion
¼ cup finely chopped green pepper

½ cup mushrooms
½ cup chopped celery
1½ pounds ground beef
Pepper
1 can tomato soup
Worcestershire sauce
Butter
Cheese, grated

Put corn and tomatoes in kettle and cook with salt and 2 tablespoons of the butter. Boil noodles, wash and drain. Melt 1 tablespoon butter in skillet and sauté onion, green pepper and mushrooms slowly until onion is clear. Add celery, meat and pepper. Cook well. Add to corn, tomatoes and tomato soup. Add Worcestershire sauce and taste for seasoning. Add noodles and simmer all together for 30 minutes. Let stand, all night if possible. One hour before serving, put mixture in buttered baking dish, dot generously with butter and grated cheese, and bake at 325° for 1 hour.

Crawford Edwards
Edwards Trust

SQUASH FILLED WITH MEAT AND RICE

12 medium-sized yellow squash
1 pound hamburger
1 large onion, chopped
½ to ¾ cup raw rice
¼ cup catsup
Salt, to taste
Pepper, to taste

¼ teaspoon cinnamon or ½ teaspoon
   allspice (not both) (optional)
Water
Oil (optional)
Tomato sauce
Juice of 1 lemon

Wash and brush squash. Cut neck of squash then scoop out center. Mix hamburger with onion, rice, catsup, salt and pepper. Add cinnamon or allspice, if desired. Add a little water. Mixture should be easy to handle. Add a little oil if meat is too lean. Stuff squash about ¾ full. Stand squash up in bottom of saucepan, add a little water and tomato sauce. Cover to cook. When it begins to cook, add lemon juice, and continue to cook over low fire for approximately 1 hour.

Al Sankary
Al's Formal Wear

AUNT HELEN'S MEAT LOAF

1½ pounds ground meat
¾ cup finely chopped onion
5 eggs
¾ cup finely crushed crackers (or
   enough to make a firm mold)

Salt, to taste
Pepper, to taste

Mix all ingredients, mold and bake at 400° for 45 minutes or until brown. Serve with the following gravy.

GRAVY
½ cup milk
1 level tablespoon flour

Salt, to taste
1 (15-ounce) can tomato juice

Blend milk, flour and salt until smooth. Add to tomato juice and heat thoroughly. Pour mixture over cooked meat loaf and heat through.

Frances Garmon
Head Coach, Women's Basketball
Texas Christian University

ROAST *REPUBLICAN* RUMP

Place one large *Republican* rump, the bigger the better (preferably Federal cut, though State or even Local will do in a pinch) in all available hot water at every opportunity. Let simmer for length of term, bring to a boil as near to election day as possible. Carve rump periodically with sharp knives, immediately thereafter rubbing in salt until it puckers. Garnish with hot rumor, spicy innuendo, and cold embarrassing facts. Consume on election night as TV dinner while watching election returns come in. If ingredients have been properly mixed, this dish is delicious. Otherwise, it may be found unusually bitter, too tough for consumption and to taste of crow.

Larry L. King
Author
"The Best Little Whorehouse in Texas"

EDITOR'S NOTE: The italicized word could be substituted with Democrat, Federal Bureaucrat, etc.

EGG & SAUSAGE CASSEROLE

6 to 8 bread slices
1 pound sausage
2 cups grated cheese
6 eggs, lightly beaten

½ cup milk
1¼ teaspoons dry mustard
1 can cream of mushroom soup
1½ cups milk

Trim crusts from bread. Place in a 13x9-inch Pyrex dish. Cook sausage until red is gone. Drain on paper towel. Put sausage on top of bread. Place cheese on top of sausage. Mix eggs, ½ cup milk and dry mustard and pour over cheese. Cover and refrigerate for 24 hours. Mix soup with 1½ cups milk and pour over casserole. Bake at 300° for 1½ hours. May be frozen.

Mrs. Tom R. Parrett (Marcia)
Wife, Mayor of San Angelo, Texas

BREAKFAST CASSEROLE

1 can crescent rolls
1 pound sausage, cooked and drained
Fresh mushrooms, sliced

¾ pound Monterey Jack cheese, grated
6 eggs, beaten
1 can cream of onion soup

Line a 13x9-inch Pyrex dish with rolls, sealing perforations. Cover with sausage, mushrooms and half the cheese. Mix eggs with soup and pour over casserole. Sprinkle remaining cheese on top. Chill overnight. Bake at 350° for 1 hour. Note: For variation, you can use cooked, crumbled bacon or bite-sized pieces of ham instead of sausage.

Mrs. Tom R. Parrett (Marcia)
Wife, Mayor of San Angelo, Texas

BUD WITH RIBS

4 pounds pork spareribs
1 (12-ounce) can or bottle Budweiser
   beer
½ cup honey

2 tablespoons lemon juice
2 teaspoons salt
1 teaspoon dry mustard
¼ teaspoon pepper

Cut spareribs into 2-rib sections. Combine remaining ingredients in a shallow glass or ceramic baking dish. Add ribs. Marinate in refrigerator for at least 24 hours, turning and basting occasionally. Arrange ribs in a single layer in a large baking pan; reserve marinade. Bake at 350° for 1½ hours, turning once and basting frequently with marinade. Note: Needless to say, you should also have a case of-ice cold Budweiser to go with the ribs. Serves 4 to 6.

Dick McMullin
Keg Restaurants

APRICOT-GLAZED PORK RIBS

5 to 6 pounds pork ribs
1 (4-ounce) bottle soy sauce

1 (12-ounce) jar apricot preserves

Wash and dry ribs. Arrange ribs in a foil-lined baking pan. Pour soy sauce over the ribs, then spread with apricot preserves. Bake at 300° for 3 hours, basting often. (Lining with foil saves washing a pan.)

Nell B. Robinson

InterFirst Bank Austin, N.A.

Allan Shivers
Senior Chairman of the Board

Dear Mr. Gardner:

I have your recent letter requesting copies of recipes that are favorites in the Shivers family.

I have enclosed several. You may use any one or all of them, as you wish.

Sincerely,

ALLAN SHIVERS

AS/bt
Encs.

 **InterFirst**

InterFirst Bank Austin, N.A.   **Allan Shivers**
                                                    Senior Chairman of the Board

Chicken Breasts Gourmet

4 chicken breasts
Flour
2 tablespoons salt
1/2 teaspoon thyme
1/2 teaspoon marjoram
1/2 teaspoon paprika
Toast
Fat for frying
Sliced almonds

Roll chicken in flour that has been seasoned with salt, thyme,
marjoram and paprika. Fry in fat until golden brown. Arrange
chicken in a roaster and cover with the following sauce. Roast
at 350 degrees for about 1 hour or until tender. Baste 2 or 3
times to glaze. Arrange chicken on toast, pour sauce over
and sprinkle with almonds to serve. (Split whole breasts in
half lengthwise)

Sauce

2 cups pineapple juice
1/4 cup lemon juice
2 tablespoons cornstarch
2 tablespoons sugar
1/2 teaspoon curry powder

Mix pineapple juice, lemon juice, cornstarch, sugar and
curry powder in a saucepan. Cook and stir until mixture
thickens slightly.

Allan Shivers

Mrs. Amon G. Carter, Jr.

Dear Russell:

The following is one of my very favorite recipes and was taken from <u>Mother Jane's Prescriptions for Hunger</u> by Jane Justin:

King Ranch Casserole

Preheat oven to 350°
Clean, boil & cut up as for chicken salad 1-3 to 4 lb. chicken
Melt in skillet...................... 2 Tbsp. Butter
Saute in butter until tender .... 1 Onion, chopped
                                     1 Clove garlic, if desired
Add .... 1 can Cream of Mushroom soup
                                     1 can Cream of Chicken soup
                                     1 can Ro-Tel Tomatoes,
                                     blend in blender
Cut into bite sized pieces.......... 1 pkg. Frozen tortillas
Dip the tortillas in hot............ Chicken stock

Place a layer of tortillas in buttered
casserole then layer of soup mixture,
then layer of chicken. Repeat tortillas,
soup mixture and chicken. Sprinkle
over top............................ 1/2 lb. sharp cheese, grated

Bake in 350° oven for 30 to 45 minutes.

Wish you much success in your endeavor.

Sincerely,

George Ann Carter

BILL ARCHER
7TH DISTRICT, TEXAS

MEMBER:
WAYS AND MEANS
COMMITTEE

Congress of the United States
House of Representatives
Washington, D.C. 20515

Chicken Divan

8 chicken breasts
2 packages frozen broccoli
1 can cream of chicken soup
1/2 cup mayonnaise
1 tablespoon lemon juice
3 tablespoons curry powder
1 cup grated cheddar cheese
seasoned breadcrumbs

Boil chicken 30 - 40 minutes until thoroughly cooked. Let
cool, and remove bones. Prepare broccoli according to
package instructions. Cover the bottom of a 9 1/2 x 13 1/2
pan with broccoli, and layer chicken breasts over the broccoli.
Make a mixture of soup, mayonnaise, lemon juice and curry
powder (use 1/2 cup of water to thin it out), and spoon over
the chicken. Top with grated cheese and breadcrumbs and
bake at 375 degrees for 20 - 30 minutes (until cheese begins
to brown)

Bill Archer
Member of Congress

Football Office

TEXAS CHRISTIAN UNIVERSITY
Fort Worth, Texas 76129

CHICKEN SPAGHETTI

Sauce: Melt ^{2}/3 Tblsp. margarine in skillet
          Saute ^{3}/4 cup onion, chopped; 1 cup chopped celery;
               ^{3}/4 cup chopped green pepper
          Add 1 Tblsp. flour, stir to thicken
          Add 1 cup chicken broth and 1 cup milk
          Add 1 can mushroom soup, sliced pimientos, and sliced olives
          Add ^{1}/2 cup margarine and cook 20 minutes

Dice cooked whole chicken.

Cook spaghetti to make 3-4 cups

In 9x13 casserole, layer sauce, spaghetti, and meat. Repeat
   layers. Top with grated cheese and cracker crumbs.

Bake at 325° approximately 45 minutes (until bubbly).

Jim Wacker

Lil Wacker

Farrah Fawcett's Chicken Marengo

3 Tbls. oil
1 - 3 1/2 lb. chicken, cut into serving pieces
1 medium onion, chopped
1/2 cup tomato puree
1 Tbls. flour
2 cups chicken stock (approx.)
1 cup dry white wine
1 clove garlic, crushed with 1 tsp. salt
2 bay leaves
1 tsp dried thyme
salt and pepper to taste
12 small white onions
1/4 lb. mushrooms
3 tomatoes
finely chopped parsley

Heat oil in a heavy casserole with a cover. Add chicken
and brown evenly all over. Add chopped onion to chicken
and cook 3 minutes.

Stir in the tomato puree and flour and mix throughly.
Gradually pour in chicken stock and wine. Add the garlic,
bay leaves, thyme, salt and pepper. Cover the casserole
and place in a preheated 350° oven for 15 minutes.

Slip white onions out of their skins. To do this easily,
put them in boiling water for 2 minutes, then slip off
the skins between finger and thumb. Cook the onions in a
saucepan until tender and add to casserole.

Wipe the mushrooms clean with a damp cloth, then slice.
Peel and quarter the tomatoes. Add mushrooms and tomatoes to the casserole and cook, covered, another 30 mins.,
until the chicken is tender. Just before serving, sprinkle
the surface with parsley. Serves 6.

WORLD'S BEST BARBECUE CHICKEN

1 whole chicken
3 to 4 bottles lemon extract

1 stick butter, melted
Barbecue seasoning (optional)

Split whole chicken in half and marinate in lemon extract for 24 hours. Chicken should be completely submerged in extract. Just before cooking, remove chicken from extract and mix extract with melted butter. Use this mixture as your basting agent. Season with barbecue seasoning, if desired. Charcoal broil chicken for 45 minutes to 1 hour, turning and basting every 10 minutes.

Charlie Hillard

WALNUT AND CHEESE STUFFED CHICKEN

4 large chicken breasts
¾ cup flour
1 egg, beaten
¾ cup bread crumbs
½ teaspoon salt
¼ teaspoon pepper
Butter for frying

1 (8-ounce) package cream cheese, softened
½ cup butter, softened
1 tablespoon parsley
½ cup chopped walnuts
2 cups grated Swiss cheese
2 cups cooked long grain and wild rice

Boil and skin chicken breasts. Roll in flour, then egg and then bread crumbs. Sprinkle with salt and pepper. Sauté in butter until lightly browned. Meanwhile, mix cream cheese with butter, parsley and walnuts. Divide into 4 egg-shaped balls and roll in Swiss cheese to coat them. Put cooked rice in casserole dish. Wrap each chicken breast around a cheese ball and place, seam side down, over rice. Bake at 350° for 15 to 20 minutes. During the last 3 minutes, top with remaining Swiss cheese. Serve hot. May be made up ahead and frozen.

Chip Moody
News Anchor
KHOU-TV
Houston, Texas

MARY GRACE'S CALABAZA CON POLLO
Mary Grace's Chicken with Squash

Cooking oil
4 chicken breasts, boned
Black pepper, to taste
Garlic powder, to taste

4 medium zucchini (5 to 7 inches long)
½ medium onion
2 medium tomatoes
1 (16-ounce) can yellow kernel corn

In large deep skillet, pour thin layer of cooking oil. Chop chicken breasts into 2-inch pieces. Cook on medium heat for about 10 minutes or until brown. Season with black pepper and garlic powder. Slice the zucchini about ½-inch thick, and then cut each slice in quarters. Allow them to cook with chicken for a couple of minutes. Dice the onion and let it brown. Dice the tomatoes and combine with remaining ingredients in skillet. Add corn, including water in can, with other ingredients. Cover and simmer for about 20 to 30 minutes. This dish should remain somewhat soupy when done. If drying, add ¼ cup water. You'll know it's done when inside of zucchini turns light green. This dish can be served as a main course or side dish.

Ron Oliveira
News Anchor
KVUE-TV
Austin, Texas

BURGUNDY CHICKEN I

2 bacon slices
1 chicken breast (about ¾ pound, split)
½ cup sliced fresh mushrooms
1 small garlic clove, minced
¼ teaspoon thyme leaves, crushed

1 (7¾-ounce) can semi-condensed tomato
    soup
¼ cup Burgundy or other dry wine
Cooked rice

In skillet, cook bacon until crisp; remove, crumble and set aside. Pour off all but 2 tablespoons drippings. Brown chicken in drippings; remove. Brown mushrooms with garlic and thyme in drippings. Blend in soup and Burgundy. Add chicken. Cover and cook over low heat for 30 minutes or until done, stirring occasionally. Serve with rice. Garnish with bacon. Serves 2.

Kim Dawson
Kim Dawson Agency

BURGUNDY CHICKEN II

6 whole chicken breasts, boned and
   halved
Flour
Salt
Pepper
Nutmeg

Cinnamon
Butter or margarine
1 large can pitted sweet cherries
2 small cans mandarin oranges
2½ cups Burgundy wine

Wash and dry chicken. Cover with flour which has been seasoned with salt, pepper, nutmeg and cinnamon. Brown in butter or margarine. Transfer to a baking dish. Cover with cherries and oranges. Make sauce of wine, cherry juice and orange juice. Cover and bake in a moderate oven until tender. Sauce may be thickened with a little flour or cornstarch, if desired.

Mr. and Mrs. Frank W. Maddox (Lucille)

HEAVEN ON A BONE
This is my absolute favorite, and it's easy to make.

Chicken breasts, skinned
Butter
Honey

Bread crumbs
Cheddar cheese, grated
Mozzarella cheese, grated

Arrange chicken breasts in a broiler pan which has been lined with foil. Brush butter and honey over chicken. Bake at 350° for 30 minutes. Mix bread crumbs with more butter. Remove chicken from oven and place crumbs on top of each chicken piece. Return to oven for 20 minutes. Sprinkle grated cheeses over chicken. (This will form a sort of skin over the chicken.) Return to oven for 10 minutes. And there you have it–Heaven On a Bone.

Neoma Salamon
News Anchor
KAMC-TV
Lubbock, Texas

CHICKEN ROSÉ
Delicious!

¼ cup soy sauce
¼ cup wine
¼ cup vegetable oil

2 tablespoons water
2 tablespoons brown sugar
4 chicken breasts

Make marinade by mixing soy sauce, wine, oil, water and brown sugar. Marinate chicken breasts overnight. Transfer chicken to casserole, pour marinade over chicken, cover casserole and bake at 350° for 1 hour.

Mr. and Mrs. Mike Gore (Linda)

BAKED CHICKEN BREASTS WITH DRIED BEEF

1 jar dried beef
4 chicken breasts, boned
4 bacon slices

1 can mushroom soup
1 cup sour cream

Arrange beef on the bottom of a baking dish. Place chicken breasts, rolled with bacon, on top. Mix soup and sour cream and pour over chicken. Bake at 350° for 2½ hours. Makes 4 servings. May be frozen.

Mrs. James C. Wright (Betty)
Wife, U. S. Congressman

BAKED CHICKEN BREASTS

6 chicken breasts
Salt, to taste
⅔ cup sliced mushrooms, sautéed
1 can mushroom soup

1 cup sour cream
½ cup cooking sherry
Paprika, to taste
Toasted slivered almonds

Season chicken breasts slightly with salt. Place chicken, skin side up, in a baking dish. Mix mushrooms, mushroom soup, sour cream and sherry and pour over chicken. Sprinkle generously with paprika. Sprinkle lightly with almonds. Bake at 350° for 1 hour or until tender. Serves 6.

Mrs. Ardell M. Young (Marjorie)

BROCCOLI CHICKEN CASSEROLE

2 (10-ounce) packages frozen broccoli
   spears, cooked and drained
1 large fryer, cooked, boned and cubed
2 cans cream of chicken soup

1 cup mayonnaise
1 teaspoon lemon juice
1 cup or more grated sharp cheese
1 cup bread crumbs, buttered

Line a greased 13x9-inch Pyrex dish with broccoli. Cover with cubed chicken. Mix undiluted soup, mayonnaise and lemon juice. Spoon over chicken. Sprinkle with cheese and top with bread crumbs. Cover and bake at 350° for 30 minutes or until done. Sliced water chestnuts can be sprinkled over chicken before soup mixture is added. This dish can be served over rice. Yields 12 lunch servings or 8 to 10 dinner servings.

Mrs. Tom R. Parrett (Marcia)
Wife, Mayor of San Angelo, Texas

CHICKEN BREASTS IN SOUR CREAM

8 to 10 strips of bacon
4 large or 6 small chicken breasts,
   boned and skinned
1 can cream of mushroom soup
   (undiluted)

½ soup can sherry
1 cup sour cream
Paprika

Cook bacon until crisp and set aside to cool. Arrange chicken breasts in shallow baking dish so the pieces do not overlap. Break bacon into bite-sized pieces and sprinkle over chicken. Combine mushroom soup, sherry and sour cream until well blended. Pour over chicken, completely covering it. Dust with paprika. Bake uncovered at 350° for 1½ hours. Serve with wild rice.

Jan Fraser, Director
Sid Richardson Collection of Western Art
Fort Worth

CHICKEN SALAD PIE
Excellent for luncheons.

2 deep dish pie crusts
2 chicken breasts, cooked, boned and
diced
3 eggs, hard-boiled and chopped
1 cup chopped celery
½ can water chestnuts, diced
½ cup mayonnaise

1 can cream of chicken soup
Salt, to taste
Pepper, to taste
Juice of ½ lemon
1 cup grated Cheddar cheese
5½ ounces potato chips, crushed

Bake pie crusts for 10 minutes and set aside. Mix chicken, eggs, celery, water chestnuts, mayonnaise, cream of chicken soup, salt, pepper and lemon juice. Pour into pie crusts. Cover with cheese and top with potato chips. Bake at 350° for 30 minutes.

Paula Zahn
News Anchor KRPC-TV
Houston, Texas
* Paula Zahn has moved to WNEV-TV, Boston

CHICKEN PINEAPPLE PIE

FILLING
2 cups diced chicken
1 cup drained pineapple

1 cup sour cream
¾ cup Miracle Whip salad dressing

Mix ingredients and refrigerate while preparing crust.

CRUST
1½ cups flour
1⅛ teaspoons salt
½ cup oil

¼ cup milk
¾ cup grated Cheddar cheese
¼ teaspoon paprika

Mix flour and salt with oil and milk. Slowly stir while adding cheese and paprika. Form into ball and press into pie pan. Bake at 400° for 10 to 15 minutes. Fill crust with chicken mixture and top with additional grated cheese. Serve cold.

Morgan Fairchild
Actress

CHICKEN SPAGHETTI

4 pounds chicken
1 cup chopped onion
1 green pepper, chopped
1 cup chopped celery
1 (16-ounce) can tomatoes
Salt, to taste
Pepper, to taste
⅛ teaspoon cayenne pepper

⅛ teaspoon paprika
Garlic or garlic salt, to taste
3 tablespoons chili powder
1 small can sliced mushrooms
1 small can tiny green peas (optional)
1 pound spaghetti
Grated Parmesan cheese

Cook chicken, bone and cut into bite-sized pieces. Dip about 3 tablespoons fat from broth, or use margarine, and heat in skillet. In this, brown onion, green pepper and celery. Stir in tomatoes, salt, pepper, cayenne pepper, paprika, garlic and chili powder. Add about 3 cups of chicken broth and cover. Simmer for about 2 hours. When almost done, add chicken, mushrooms and green peas and allow to simmer a few more minutes. Cook spaghetti according to package directions. Combine with meat sauce. Allow at least 30 minutes for the spaghetti to absorb all the juices. Serve with Parmesan cheese sprinkled on top. Note: The sauce can be made ahead and frozen. Serves 16 to 20.

Mrs. Dan Goldsmith (Grace)

CRUNCHY CHICKEN BAKE

2 cups crushed Triscuits
2 (10¾-ounce) cans cream of chicken
   soup
½ cup salad dressing
2 cups diced chicken
2 (10½-ounce) cans asparagus spears,
   drained

1 (8-ounce) can water chestnuts, drained
   and sliced
2 (2½-ounce) jars mushrooms, drained
¼ cup margarine, melted

Spread half the crushed wafers in a greased 13x9-inch pan. Mix soup and salad dressing and carefully spread half the mixture over the wafers. Top with chicken, asparagus, water chestnuts and mushrooms. Spread remaining mix on top. Top with remaining crushed Triscuits. Drizzle melted margarine over Triscuits. Cover loosely with foil and bake at 350° for 30 minutes. Uncover and bake for 15 minutes. Makes 8 servings. May be frozen.

Mrs. Ron Paul (Carol)
Wife, U. S. Congressman

KING RANCH CHICKEN

1 (3-pound) fryer
12 corn tortillas
1 can cream of chicken soup
1 can cream of mushroom soup

1½ teaspoons chili powder
1 can Ro-Tel tomatoes
¼ pound Cheddar cheese, grated

Cook chicken and reserve broth. Bone chicken and cut into bite-sized pieces. Tear tortillas in pieces and dip in chicken broth. Cover the bottom of a 13x9-inch casserole with a layer of tortillas. Add a layer of chicken. In a separate bowl, mix soups, chili powder and tomatoes. Pour a layer of sauce over chicken. Repeat layers of tortillas, chicken and sauce. Top with cheese. Bake at 350° for 30 minutes.

Mrs. Ken Armbrister (Susie)
Wife, State Representative

PINEAPPLE CHICKEN PASTA SALAD

2 cups cooked diced chicken
1 small box pasta shells, cooked and
   cooled
2 tablespoons crushed pineapple
2 teaspoons soy sauce
¼ cup chopped green pepper

1 teaspoon finely diced onion or
   scallions
Mayonnaise, to taste
Dash ginger
½ cup chopped pecans (optional)

Combine all ingredients and chill thoroughly. Will keep for several days in the refrigerator.

Mrs. Mickey Leland (Alison Walton)
Wife, U. S. Congressman

LLOYD BENTSEN

TEXAS

United States Senate

WASHINGTON, D.C. 20510

Dear Mr. Gardner:

The attached material is forwarded in response to your recent request. If you need further information or assistance, please do not hesitate to contact me again.

Thank you for contacting my office.

Sincerely,

Lloyd Bentsen

Enclosure

LLOYD BENTSEN

TEXAS

𝔘nited 𝔖tates 𝔖enate

WASHINGTON, D.C. 20510

Baked Crab in Shell

1 cup diced onion
2 cups diced celery
1 green pepper, diced
butter
1 cup cracker crumbs
1 pint table cream
Tabasco sauce, to taste
Lea and Perrins Worcestershire sauce, to taste
Parsley
1 pound lump crab
Paprika
Lemon, to garnish

Saute onion, celery and green pepper in butter. In bowl,
mix cracker crumbs, cream, Tabasco sauce, Worcestershire
sauce and parsley. Add sauteed vegetables and crab meat.
Fill crab shells and top with paprika. Bake at 350 degrees
for 40 minutes. Garnish with lemon.

Lloyd Bentsen

LBJ Ranch

Stonewall, Texas

Mrs Lyndon B. Johnson's recipe for

SHRIMP SQUASH CASSEROLE

1-1/2 lbs. yellow squash=3 cups yellow squash
3/4 cups raw shrimp
2T. butter
2T. flour
1/2 t. salt
1/8 tsp. black pepper
1 cup chicken broth (use bouillon cube)
1/2 cup whipping cream or small can chilled milk
1 T. instant minced onion
1/2 cup coarse bread crumbs
1/4 cup grated parmesan cheese
1 T. butter

1. Wash and dry squash. Cut crosswise into 1/4 inch slices.
2. Thoroughly rinse shrimp under cold water. Drain.
3. Heat the 2 T. butter in sauce pan. Blend in flour, salt & pepper.
   Cook until it bubbles.
4. Remove from heat and add chicken broth gradually stirring constantly.
   Bring to boil for 1 or 2 mins.
5. Blend in cream and minced onions. Mix in the raw shrimp.
6. Put in layer of squash in bottom of a 1-1/2 qt. casserole and
   spoon half of the shrimp sauce over squash. Repeat layer with
   remaining squash and shrimp sauce.
7. Cover tightly and set in a 400 degree oven for 30 mins.
8. Meanwhile, toss crumbs and Parmesan cheese with melted butter.
9. After 30 mins., remove casserole from oven and reduce heat to
   350 degrees. Remove cover and top with bread crumbs. Return
   to oven 15 mins. or until crumbs are golden brown.

**CBS
NEWS**
A Division of CBS Inc

Herring Copenhagen

1 dozen herring filets in brine
1 whole herring in brine
1 cup distilled white vinegar
1/2 cup finely granulated sugar
1/4 tsp. ground allspice
1/2 tsp. ground white pepper
4 bay leaves
1/2 cup coarsley chopped Bermuda onion

Place herring in a large enamel or earthenware bowl.
Add cold water to cover. Soak herring overnight to
remove excess salt, changing water several times.
Drain herring. Cut each filet crosswise into 1-inch
pieces. Prepare whole herring in similar manner.
Place in separate bowl. Place remaining ingredients
in saucepan, bring to a boil and simmer 1 minute.
Remove from heat and cool to room temperature.
Pour most of the marinade over the fileted pieces.
Pour remainder over whole herring pieces. Cover
bowls and let herring marinate in refrigerator for
6 hours or longer. Drain, reserve marinade.
Serve herring plain, using pieces cut from whole
herring as garnish, or use in many ways for main
dish or salad offerings.   Serves 25.

Walter Cronkite

SAUTÉED CRAB MEAT WITH CURRY AND ALMONDS

¾ cup sliced toasted almonds
2 tablespoons oil
5 tablespoons butter
¼ cup finely chopped onion or green
  onion
¼ cup finely chopped green pepper
1 to 3 tablespoons curry powder
  (according to individual taste)

1 teaspoon chili powder
1 pound lump crab meat
1 cup heavy cream
1 teaspoon salt
Rice ring
¼ cup chopped parsley

Place almonds on an oiled baking pan or cookie sheet and toast briefly in a 350° oven, stirring frequently, until they are lightly browned and crisp. Set aside to cool. Heat the oil and butter in a 9-inch skillet and, when fairly hot, add the onion and green pepper. Let them cook several minutes over medium heat. Add the curry powder and chili powder and mix well. When the pepper and onion are somewhat tenderized, but not browned, add the crab meat and toss until merely heated through. Add the cream and salt and let mixture blend well and cook through. If the crab absorbs too much cream and the mixture looks dry, add more cream. Meanwhile, cook the rice, put into a buttered ring mold, unmold onto a hot platter. Spoon the crab mixture into the center and top with chopped parsley and toasted almonds. Serve with chutney. Bananas baked in their skins are also excellent with this dish.

Denton A. Cooley, M.D.
Surgeon-in-Chief
Texas Heart Institute
Houston, Texas

SHRIMP DE JONGHE

1 cup butter, melted
2 garlic cloves, minced
⅓ cup chopped parsley
½ teaspoon paprika
Dash cayenne pepper

⅔ cup cooking sherry
2 cups soft bread crumbs
5 to 6 cups cleaned cooked shrimp (4
  pounds in shell)
Additional chopped parsley, to garnish

To melted butter, add garlic, parsley, paprika, cayenne pepper and sherry; mix well. Add bread crumbs and toss. Place shrimp in 11x7-inch baking dish. Spoon the butter mixture over shrimp. Bake at 325° for 20 to 25 minutes or until crumbs brown. Sprinkle with additional chopped parsley before serving. Serves 6 to 8.

Mrs. Ardell M. Young (Marjorie)

SHRIMP CREOLE

1 green pepper, chopped
3 garlic cloves, finely diced
2 onions, chopped
Butter
3 cans tomato sauce
3 cans water
1 teaspoon parsley

¼ teaspoon thyme
Salt, to taste
Pepper, to taste
2 pounds headless shrimp (4 pounds
  with heads)
Cornstarch

Sauté green pepper, garlic and onions in a little butter until brown. Mix tomato sauce, water, parsley, thyme, salt and pepper in a saucepan. Stir in sautéed pepper, garlic and onions. Cook sauce for 30 minutes, then add shrimp, 1 at a time. Thicken with cornstarch when ready to serve. Prepare hours ahead of time and let sit so spices will go through shrimp. Serve on rice. Serves 4.

Mrs. Joan Kline

GRANDMA'S SHRIMP CREOLE

⅔ cup fat (bacon drippings)
¾ cup flour, sifted
2 cups chopped onion
1 cup chopped green pepper
¼ cup chopped celery
1 (8-ounce) can tomato sauce
2 pounds cleaned shrimp

2 teaspoons salt
½ teaspoon black pepper
¼ teaspoon red pepper
1 cup or more hot water
1½ tablespoons chopped parsley
1½ tablespoons chopped green onion
  tops

Make a golden brown mixture of fat and flour. Add onion, pepper and celery and cook slowly until clear, stirring frequently. Add tomato sauce and cook over low heat for 20 minutes. Add shrimp, salt, black and red pepper. If mixture becomes dry, add hot water. Cook 10 minutes longer. Add parsley and onion tops. Serve on rice. Will serve 10 nicely.

Charles Mayberry

CREAMED COCONUT SHRIMP

1½ pounds shrimp
Butter
Garlic

1 can frozen coconut milk (found in
Oriental stores)
Onion tops

Clean and devein raw shrimp. Place butter in large skillet. Add diced garlic and sauté shrimp about 8 to 10 minutes or until shrimp are white in color. Add the coconut milk. cover and simmer on low heat about 10 to 15 minutes. Add chopped onion tops just before done. For variation, add ½ cup pineapple chunks. Serve with rice.

Angelo George
Angelo's Bar-B-Que

SCAMPI BOCA

6 shrimp per person
Light oil
1 teaspoon butter
¼ cup brandy
½ teaspoon garlic

Fresh cream
1 tablespoon butter
Salt, to taste
Pepper, to taste

Sauté the shrimp in light oil and a teaspoon of butter. When the shrimp are half cooked, add the brandy, garlic and fresh cream. When the cream is reduced by half, add 1 tablespoon butter and blend thoroughly. Add salt and pepper, to taste. Serve with saffron rice. Note: This shrimp dish was created at the famed 5 star resort, the Boca Raton Hotel and Club. It was here where I maintained the position of gourmet chef in the Top of the Tower Restaurant.

Patrick R. Nitto
Executive Chef
Americana Hotel

PAPAYA SHRIMP ROYALE

Papaya, halved
San Francisco baby shrimp
Chopped chives

Chopped celery
Dressing (your choice)

Fill papaya halves with shrimp. Top with chives, celery and your choice of dressing.

Ruta Lee
Actress

DALE'S DIVINITY SHRIMP

An elegant but easy dish that any Texas cook would be proud to serve!

SHRIMP STOCK

2 cups water
Shells from 1 pound of shrimp

1 tablespoon salt
½ pound shrimp, puréed

Simmer water, shrimp shells and salt over low heat until reduced to 1 cup of liquid. Remove shells and add the puréed shrimp.

DIVINITY SAUCE

1 pound jumbo shrimp, sautéed
1 pound sour cream
1 teaspoon paprika
1 teaspoon cayenne pepper
1 cup reduced shrimp stock (see above)

1 tablespoon salt
¾ cup chives
¾ cup sliced fresh mushrooms

Mix ingredients and heat in a saucepan over low heat, stirring frequently. When sufficiently heated, serve immediately on a bed of white rice. Note: This dish looks lovely when served in a porcelain rarebit dish, garnished with fresh sliced mushrooms and chives. Serves 4.

Dale Emmert
Debra Emmert
Capitol Oyster Bar
Austin

SHRIMP REMOULADE

4 tablespoons olive oil
2 tablespoons vinegar
1 teaspoon salt
2 teaspoons Creole mustard
6 small green onions, minced

2 celery stalks, minced
Few drops Tabasco sauce
¼ teaspoon paprika
Boiled shrimp

Make French dressing by mixing all ingredients except shrimp. Pour over shrimp. Let stand in refrigerator for 4 to 5 hours before serving. Serve on shredded lettuce as a first course.

Dawn Queen McDavid
David McDavid Pontiac - GMC - Honda

SCALLOPS BAKED IN GARLIC SAUCE

2 pounds bay scallops or sea scallops, halved
3 garlic cloves, covered with boiling water
1 cup butter

½ cup or more sliced mushrooms
¼ teaspoon salt
⅛ teaspoon pepper
¼ cup fine bread crumbs

Wipe scallops. Drain garlic and mash or pound them in butter until well-blended. Lightly grease a small casserole with part of the garlic butter. Add mushrooms. Arrange scallops over mushrooms. Dot with all but 2 tablespoons of remaining garlic butter. Mix salt, pepper and bread crumbs and sprinkle over scallops. Bake at 350° for 10 to 22 minutes or until browned. For individual service, bake in small scallop shells or ramekins. Yields 6 servings.

Mrs. Heywood Clemons (Harriett)

TUNA ITALIAN

½ cup chopped onion
Fat
1 can cream of mushroom soup
1 (6-ounce) can evaporated milk or ⅔ cup light cream
⅓ cup grated Parmesan cheese
1 (7 or 9¼-ounce) can tuna, drained
1 (3-ounce) can broiled, sliced mushrooms, drained

6 ounces noodles, cooked
½ cup chopped ripe olives
2 tablespoons minced parsley
2 teaspoons lemon juice
Additional grated Parmesan cheese
Paprika
Parsley, to garnish
Ripe olive slices, to garnish

Cook onion in small amount of hot fat until tender but not brown. Add soup, milk and cheese; heat and stir. Break tuna in chunks and add to soup mixture with mushrooms, noodles, olives, parsley and lemon juice. Mix well. Pour into greased 2-quart casserole. Sprinkle with additional Parmesan cheese and paprika. Bake at 375° for 20 to 25 minutes. Garnish with additional parsley and olive slices. Serves 6.

Ellen Terry
Realtor

NANCY'S GUMBO

¾ cup uncooked rice
2 (14½-ounce) cans clear chicken broth
1 (14-ounce) can whole tomatoes
1 onion, diced
1 (6½-ounce) can tuna, packed in oil (do not drain)

1 box frozen whole okra
2 heaping tablespoons gumbo filé
Cayenne pepper, to taste
Celery seed, to taste
Black pepper, to taste

Cook rice in salted water; drain. Add chicken broth, tomatoes, onion, undrained tuna, okra and gumbo filé. Sprinkle top well with cayenne pepper, celery seed and black pepper. Bring mixture to a boil. Add extra salt and pepper, to taste. Note: The taste improves the following day. Serves 6 to 8.

Mr. and Mrs. James Hagood (Nancy)

BAKED TROUT, RED SNAPPER OR BASS

1 (14 to 16-inch) trout, red snapper or bass
3 to 4 fresh onions, sliced
Butter
Garlic salt, to taste

Salt, to taste
Black pepper, to taste
1 to 1½ ounces or more red wine
1 lemon

Place fish on large piece of heavy foil. Put 2 or 3 fresh onions inside and 1 out. Add a pat of butter inside and out. Sprinkle well with garlic salt, salt and black pepper. Add wine. Squeeze lemon over fish, then drop the rind into package. Carefully wrap fish in foil (sprayed with vegetable spray.) Bake over hot coals or in a 450° oven for 30 minutes on 1 side, turn and bake 15 more minutes. Open and enjoy.

Preston Smith
Governor of Texas
1969-1972

Mrs. Rita Weick,
King Ranch,

Dear Mr. Gardner,

　　How nice of you to think of including King
Ranch in your 'Cookbook'. I am sorry to be so
late in sending these recipes, but you caught us
at a very busy time here.

　　My husband, Gerhard Weick, is Manager of the
Main Residence and also an avid cook. The Venison
recipe is one of his favourites. As you are probably
aware South Texas abounds in deer. The Hot Sauce
is made in our Main Residence kitchen by Richard
Gonzales. He has been with the Ranch for more than
30 years.

　　I hope these recipes will be of interest to
you and I am looking forward to receiving a copy
of your book. We both wish you all the best on
your endeavour.

　　　　　　　　　Sincerely,

Kingsville, Kleberg Co., Tex.

TEXAS DOVE RECIPE

Obtain a good dove lease or acquire acreage that attracts dove. When September 1st arrives each year, obtain some of your closest friends and substantial refreshments to engage in the hunt. Arrive at the hunting scene and place your friends at least 200 yards away, since most of them are probably dangerous with a gun. Proceed to shoot dove, but not beyond limits set each year by the Texas Parks and Wildlife Commission. Have your friends clean the dove while you appear busy straightening up the area where the hunt was conducted. After obtaining the largest number of birds possible that can be negotiated with your friends, take the birds home and have them properly cleaned. Using only the dove breast, simmer a pan of milk and place the number of dove you desire to cook into the pan and allow the dove to simmer in the milk for approximately 2 to 3 minutes. Remove the dove from the pan and place two of the dove breasts together with half of a jalapeño pepper between the two breasts. Wrap the two breasts with bacon and secure with toothpicks. Depending on the weather, the birds may then be baked or charcoal-broiled with your favorite barbecue sauce applied to the birds. The jalapeno pepper will flavor the birds. The milk tenderizes the birds and the bacon sweetens the flavor to remove any wild taste.

Lyndell Kirkley
Attorney at Law

MOURNING DOVE MANGIAMELE

Doves   Bacon

Clean dove. Wrap dove in bacon strip, and secure with toothpicks. Place on a charcoal grill. Remove when done. Enjoy! Chew slowly, as shotgun pellets may be present. Note: This is a very simple recipe which may be used at the end of a day of dove hunting. Fancy recipes are difficult while afield, but this one is a "no brainer," easily and quickly prepared.

Mr. and Mrs. Paul Mangiamele (Lisa)

SUSAN'S SPECIAL DOVE

Dove   Water
Butter   4 tablespoons vinegar
Garlic salt   6 tablespoons barbecue sauce
Onion (optional)

Tear pieces of foil for every 2 dove. Place 2 dove in center of foil. Put a pat of butter on top of dove and sprinkle with garlic salt. If desired, place onion on top. Seal the dove in tight little packages. Place these packages on a rack in a pan. Fill the bottom of the pan with an inch of water mixed with vinegar and barbecue sauce. Cover and seal the whole pan with foil. Bake at 325° for 1½ hours. Then enjoy!

Mr. and Mrs. David Irvin (Susan)

DOVE BREASTS STROGANOFF

12 to 18 dove breasts (remove legs)
1 medium onion, chopped
2 tablespoons butter, melted
1 (10¾-ounce) can cream of celery soup
1 (4-ounce) can mushrooms
½ cup sauterne wine
½ teaspoon oregano

½ teaspoon rosemary
Salt, to taste
Pepper, to taste
1 teaspoon bottled brown bouquet sauce
1 cup sour cream
Cooked wild rice
Brandied peaches

Arrange dove breasts in large baking dish. Do not crowd. Sauté onion in butter. Add remaining ingredients except sour cream, rice and peaches. Pour mixture over dove breasts. Cover lightly with foil. Bake at 325° for 1 hour, turning occasionally. Stir in sour cream. Bake, uncovered, for 20 minutes. To serve, spoon over rice and accompany with brandied peaches. Serves 6 to 9.

Electra Waggoner Biggs
W. T. Waggoner Estate

LAREDO CHILI
First place winner in Congressional Club Chili Cook-off.

3 pounds ground venison, chili cut
2 pounds ground beef, chili cut
2 large sweet onions, chopped
2 large garlic cloves, minced
1 (15-ounce) can Spanish style tomato
  sauce (Town House brand)
1 (8-ounce) glass jar Old El Paso hot
  taco sauce

1 (4-ounce) package Adkins Texas style
  seasoning
3 (15-ounce) cans water
1 can tomato soup
1 can Texas Lone Star or Pearl beer

In a heavy skillet or boiler, sauté venison and beef until light. When cooked, add and sauté onions and garlic. Add tomato sauce, taco sauce and Adkins seasoning, and simmer on low for 30 minutes, stirring often and adding water as you go along. Continue simmering for another hour on low heat. Add soup for thickening. Dilute soup with the beer. Note: The taco sauce comes in mild, medium or hot. Suit your taste.

Mrs. Abraham Kazen, Jr.
Wife, U. S. Congressman

BARBECUED DUCK

Duck(s)
½ stick butter
½ lemon

½ teaspoon crystallized ginger
1 cup barbecue sauce

Dress ducks and, if possible, leave skin on duck to protect the meat from drying. Preheat oven to 325°. Lay out a sheet of aluminum foil large enough to make a pouch for the duck. Place duck in center of foil. Put butter inside duck. Squeeze lemon over duck. Sprinkle ginger over the duck. Pour barbecue sauce over duck, covering it. Now, form a pouch around the duck leaving a loose fit and making sure that the pouch is sealed similar to wrapping on a baked potato. Place the pouch with the duck in the roasting pan. Do this for each duck. When finished, pour a quarter of an inch of water in the bottom of the pan, cover the pan, place in oven and cook for 2½ hours. Note: If the ducks are small as is the case with teal, you can place 2 ducks in the same pouch. Also, check the ducks each hour to make sure they are not drying out. If they are, add more sauce.

John S. Howell, IV

SOUPED UP MALLARD

4 to 6 mallard duck breasts
Salt, to taste
Pepper, to taste
Garlic salt, to taste
Vegetable oil
½ cup chopped onion
2 cans cream of mushroom soup
1 can golden mushroom soup

1 cup water
1 cup milk
¼ cup Worcestershire sauce
8 drops Tabasco sauce
1 cup chopped fresh mushrooms
1 orange
1 cup Burgundy wine

Cut duck breasts in half, or you can bone them out. Season with salt, pepper and garlic salt. Brown in vegetable oil. Cook onion in with the duck. In a separate saucepan, make mushroom soup gravy. Over low heat mix mushroom soup and golden mushroom soup. Add water, milk, Worcestershire sauce, Tabasco sauce, salt and pepper. Mix well. Add gravy to duck and bake at 375° for 2 hours. Stir in chopped mushrooms. Slice orange and lay slices on top of duck and gravy. Bake another hour or until tender. When tender, add Burgundy wine. Serve with rice.

Skeet George
Angelo's Bar-B-Que

CURRIED QUAIL

4 tablespoons butter
4 tablespoons flour
½ teaspoon salt
2 cups milk
1 teaspoon curry
½ teaspoon (Wyler's chicken bouillon)
1½ cups cooked quail breast

Wild rice
Raisins
Bananas, diced
Apples, diced
Onions, diced
Eggs, hard-boiled and diced
Nuts, chopped

Melt butter in a large saucepan, stir in flour and salt and cook until bubbly. Slowly add milk and stir briskly. Then add curry, bouillon and cooked quail or dove. Cook until flavors are blended. Serve over wild rice. Sprinkle with condiments such as raisins, bananas, apples, onions, eggs and nuts. Serves 6.

Mr. and Mrs. David Irvin (Susan)

FRIED WILD TURKEY

Breast of turkey (domestic turkey may
  be substituted)
Salt, to taste
Pepper, to taste

2½ cups or more buttermilk
2 cups vegetable oil
Flour

Bone the breast of turkey. Slice the breast in ¼-inch thick slices or thicker, if desired. Salt and pepper to taste. Soak turkey slices in buttermilk for 2 to 3 minutes. While turkey is soaking, heat vegetable oil in frying pan. Roll turkey slices in flour. Drop in heated oil (327°) and fry until golden brown. (Do not overcook.) Drain on a paper towel. Best served with cream gravy.

Mrs. Madeline Russell
Walter Russell Ranch

The newly renovated Tarrant County Courthouse, Sundance Square, and City Center Tower bring together the "old" and the "new" in Fort Worth, Texas. The Tarrant County Courthouse was constructed in 1893 and is representative of courthouses across the state. The area surrounding the structure is known as Sundance Square. The buildings have been restored to resemble the area during the days of Butch Cassidy and the Sundance Kid when Fort Worth, as it is today, was referred to as "Cowtown." The modern glass City Center Tower was completed in 1982 and was designed by Paul Rudolph, chairman, Yale School of Architecture.

DAVEY O'BRIEN EDUCATIONAL AND CHARITABLE TRUST

My Favorite Recipe:
 Legal Rice.

8 oz Long Rice, cooked and allowed to cool.
½ oz Salt   5 oz Baby Bay Shrimp
3 oz Chopped Black Olives   1 Tablespoon chopped fresh dill
2 hard boiled eggs.   1 oz Capers
2 oz Red Wine Vinegar   3 oz Olive Oil

Assemble in a large bowl, the rice, shrimp,
olives, dill. capers and salt. Toss them lightly.
mix the oil and Vinegar and sprinkle over.
Toss it again and decorate with sliced hard
boiled egg. Chill for one hour and serve

Yield   4 Salads

Charles Ringler

GIBSON D. (GIB) LEWIS

Dear Mr. Gardner,

Thank you so much for your request of favorite recipes. Enclosed
please find two that I have used for many special and not so special
occasions for a number of years.

As you may notice I especially love good and easy recipes because I
don't like to go to a lot of trouble for a meal or dessert.

I hope you can use them and again I appreciate your interest.

Best regards,

Sandra E. Lewis

Marinated Carrots

2 lbs. cooked carrots
1 bell pepper
1 medium onion, sliced into rings
1 can tomato soup
1/4 cup oil
1 cup sugar
1 Tbsp. dry mustard
3/4 cup vinegar
1 tsp. salt

Layer alternately hot carrots, pepper and onion.

Bring remaining ingredients to a boil and pour over carrots. May be served hot, but better if refrigerated overnight.

Sandra E. Lewis

Mr. Gardner:

Here is my favorite recipe, which was developed by my father when he was a rancher in South Texas in the 1930's:

ANDY MARROU'S FAMOUS BEANS

Soak one-pound package of beans overnight in 3 quarts of water, with one teaspoon salt. Pour off dirty water in the morning, add another 3 quarts of clean water.

1 small jar Pace's Picante sauce, medium flavor
1 pound bacon, chopped up
1 pound ham, small cubes
1/2 teaspoon garlic salt

Cook on low for 6 to 7 hours, then add garlic salt to taste. Beans actually get more flavorful after a day or so in the refrigerator. Have never failed to be the hit of any barbecue. Beans can be frozen and microwaved.

Sincerely,

Chris Marrou

HARTE-HANKS COMMUNICATIONS INC.
A CBS AFFILIATE

State of Texas
House of Representatives
W. Tip Hall Jr.

Dear Mr. Gardner:

Thanks for the opportunity to submit recipes for your
book. I think this is a great idea, too. My recipe
 is as follows:

Corn Casserole

2 cans shoepeg corn drained
2 cans Veg-All drained
1 cup grated cheddar cheese
1 chopped onion
   Melt together
3/4 cup mayonnaise
1 stick garlic cheese
1 stick jalapeno cheese
   Pour over vegetables combining
all ingredients. Place in greased
casserole dish adding 1 stick
margarine. Dot with cheese balls.
Bake 20 minutes at 350°.

Good luck with your book.

Sincerely,

Tip Hall

The Texas Senate

JOHN T. MONTFORD
STATE SENATOR
DISTRICT 28

P. O. BOX 12068
AUSTIN, TEXAS 78711
512/475-0176

COMMITTEES:
EDUCATION
JURISPRUDENCE
  SUBCOMMITTEE
  ON CRIMINAL MATTERS
NATURAL RESOURCES
  VICE CHAIRMAN,
  SUBCOMMITTEE ON
  WATER

Dear Russell:

Enclosed, as requested, is one of my favorite recipes, Corn Casserole.

Good luck with your book. I will look forward to receiving a copy, upon completion.

Corn Casserole

2 cans corn (drained)
1 can (4 oz.) chopped green chilies (regular)
4 oz cream cheese
1/4 cup milk
1 Tbsp. butter
dash garlic salt
pinch black pepper

Combine all ingredients in baking dish. Bake, uncovered, approx. 25 mins. at 350°.

If I can ever be of help to you in the Texas Senate, please let me know.

Yours very truly,

JOHN T. MONTFORD

lw

BROOKSHIRE GROCERY CO.

TIM BROOKSHIRE
DIRECTOR OF PERSONNEL

BUFFET VEGETABLE BAKE

2 green peppers
2 cups frozen French style
   green beans, packed
2 cups frozen baby lima beans,
   packed
2 cups frozen green peas

1 cup heavy cream
1 cup mayonnaise
3/4 cup cheese, half Parmesan
   & half cheddar, packed
   salt & pepper

Wash and seed green peppers, cut into thin strips and blanch to
destroy the bitter flavor. Place green pepper strips and
vegetables in layers in a heavily buttered shallow 2 quart
casserole. Whip cream and fold in mayonnaise, cheeses and spices.
Cover vegetables with whipped cream mixture and sprinkle with
additional parmesan cheese. Hold in refrigerator unitl ready to
bake. Bake at 325° F. for 50 minutes, or until puffed and golden
brown. Serves 12

City of Lufkin

LUFKIN, TEXAS

PITSER H. GARRISON
MAYOR

Dear Mr. Gardner,

Since Carrots are one of the big vegetable crops of Texas I am enclosing a good recipe from my wife's collection.   I am by no means a cook, but I like good food.

Also, I am enclosing a pecan pie recipe that has been in my wife's recipe collection for many, many years, and her mother's collection for fifty or more years before.   This recipe is also a real Texas treat.

Good luck to you.

Yours truly,

Pitser H. Garrison

Pitser H. Garrison

PITSER H. GARRISON
MAYOR

Escalloped Carrots

10 Carrots
1 cup Milk
3 Eggs beaten
1 med. onion chopped fine
1 cup fine bread crumbs
1/4 cup melted butter
Salt and Pepper

Boil carrots in small amount of water until tender. Mash
and add all other ingredients. Salt and pepper to taste;
add a very small amount of sugar if desired. Mix well,
put in buttered baking dish. Place dish in pan of water.
Bake until firm in moderate oven - about one hour.

Pitser H. Garrison

Dear Mr. Gardner:

It was kind of you to invite me to contribute a recipe to your Sesquicentennial cookbook.

I'm enclosing my effort. This may be in a little different style than most recipes--but then, I am too.

I hope your project is a big success.

Sincerely,

BOB BULLOCK
Comptroller of Public Accounts

BB:gcc

enclosure

BROWN BEANS BY BULLOCK

It ought not be necessary to have a recipe for cooking a pot of pinto beans. But it must be. I've come to that conclusion after the many times I've been served mushy pintos that don't even deserve to be recycled on a nacho.

Soaking beans overnight is the Number One killer of a good pot of beans. Don't do it. This old soaking overnight mistake is a hangover from the days when beans were sold in bulk straight from the fields without washing. Today's packaged beans are free of dirt and rocks and need only a little rinsing.

The second enemy of a good pot of pintos is cooking them too long in the name of making them just soft enough to eat. How *long* they cook isn't the answer–*how* they cook is.

Put your beans in a pot and cover them at least three times higher with water. Bring to a rapid boil for five minutes covered. After five minutes of boil, turn out the fire and DO NOT OPEN THE LID. If you open the lid, forget it. You've ruined it.

Let the covered pot set for one hour. Then turn the fire back on just a little higher than a simmer. When the pot starts boiling again and the lid starts jumping around and sputtering over on the stove, put in a tablespoon of oil. This will cut down the sputtering.

After a couple of hours–a little longer if you're busy doing something else–you should need to add more water. Add only *hot* water. Never put cold water in a boiling food.

This is also a good time to add some onion, a slab of salt pork or whatever else you like. The salt pork sold in most markets today is so sorry that you get about the same good out of a couple of strips of bacon.

Now turn the fire down to simmer and let's thicken the juice. A tablespoon or two of brown sugar works fine. It doesn't taste in the beans. Some folks like to use two or three tablespoons of masa flour worked into a paste. You can taste this in the beans–but it is good. Incidentally, if you don't keep masa flour around, you can get the same effect by pulverizing a handful of Fritos.

Now the beans can simmer until they are exactly like you want them. They will not get mushy.

At this point you can also decide if you want just plain beans or if you want to go another route. If you like something off in the sweet direction, put in some more brown sugar or a little molasses.

If you want something with a little zing, put in whatever is your favorite of barbecue sauce, steak sauce, chili powder, jalapeños or the like.

When all this is simmered in good, you're ready to eat. If you're planning ahead, you can now put the beans in the icebox and warm 'em up when ready. Just warm them; don't cook 'em to death and they won't get mushy but the juice will get thick.

Bob Bullock
Comptroller of Public Accounts

Sports Illustrated

TIME & LIFE BUILDING
NEW YORK, N.Y. 10020
212 JU 6-1212

NAVY BEANS FOR WRITERS

You get you two sacks of dried Navy beans
and put 'em in the biggest pot you can find
and run hot water on 'em till they drowned.
Cover 'em with pepper till they about half-
choked. Cut up garlic and onions and add
more pepper. Many people don't add enough
black pepper. Then find you a hambone or
at least a pound of bacon and cook it till
it's greasier than your hair and then dump
the whole &#!/@ in the pot, grease and all,
and add more pepper.

Smoke some cigarettes while you bring all
this to a boil, then turn the stove down
low and let them sumbitches cook for about
two or three hours, after which you got you
some Navy beans for writers what you can eat
on for two or three days while you write your
books. A man who can cook his own beans don't
hardly need to ask anybody anything about
nothing.

Dan Jenkins

ITALIAN STUFFED ARTICHOKES

4 cups bread crumbs
4 cups grated Romano cheese
5 large garlic cloves, finely chopped
4 artichokes

Salt, to taste
Pepper, to taste
4 small pieces salt pork
1 cup olive oil

Make stuffing by mixing bread crumbs, cheese and garlic. Cut tops off artichokes and spread leaves apart. Fill with stuffing as much as each artichoke will hold. Place in large Dutch oven with enough water in bottom to touch bottom leaves. Salt and pepper the top of artichokes. Place salt pork in each artichoke and pour ¼ cup olive oil over each. Bring water to a boil and cover. Cook over medium heat until a leaf can be easily extracted. You may need to add more water to bottom of pan. Do not let pan go dry. Remove and serve hot or cold.

Ray Petta

GLADYS' BAKED BEANS
Award winner!

2 bacon slices
⅛ cup diced white onion
1 tablespoon catsup
½ teaspoon mustard

1 tablespoon brown sugar
1 tablespoon white Karo syrup
1 (1-pound) can Stokely VanKamp Pork
    and Beans

Fry bacon in a 1-quart saucepan until fully cooked. Add onion and allow onion to soften and brown slightly. Add catsup, mustard, brown sugar and Karo syrup, and allow to heat to just below boil. Then add the beans. Bake at 350° for 30 minutes or at full power in microwave for 10 minutes. Note: My first brush with fame came at age 8, when, in 1955 my mother was awarded the Stokely VanKamp Outstanding Cook Award. She was photographed by the *Star-Telegram* with her three sons and later interviewed by WBAP-TV. When the *Telegram* ran the photograph the next day, there were her three sons by her side. The fame was fleeting, but we have enjoyed the recipe all these years. I hope you enjoy it, too.

Roger D. Latham

BROCCOLI-CELERY CASSEROLE

1 cup instant rice
1 package frozen chopped broccoli
1 large onion, diced
½ cup diced celery
Butter

1 can mushroom soup
½ cup milk
1 small jar Cheez Whiz
Dash paprika

Prepare rice and broccoli according to package directions. Sauté onion and celery in butter until brown. Add mushroom soup, milk and Cheez Whiz. Place alternate layers of rice and broccoli in a 2-quart casserole. Pour onion mixture over rice and broccoli. Sprinkle with paprika. Bake at 350° for 15 to 20 minutes or until cheese is bubbly. Serves 4 to 6.

Mrs. Sam Jackson (Faye)

CELERY CASSEROLE

1 celery stalk
1 large green pepper
Salt, to taste

1 can cream of mushroom or chicken
   soup
1 cup grated sharp cheese

Wash and clean celery; remove leaves. Cut diagonally into 1-inch pieces. Wash pepper and cut into bite-sized pieces. Cook celery and pepper in small amount of salted water until tender. Stir in soup and grated cheese. Cover and heat until cheese melts and sauce is thoroughly heated. Do not overcook. Serve at once.

Nell B. Robinson

MANDARIN CARROTS

5 pounds carrots, sliced ½-inch thick
1 gallon water
2 whole cloves
8 ounces brown sugar

¼ teaspoon salt
⅛ teaspoon white pepper
8 ounces margarine
1 medium orange, sliced paper-thin and
   quartered

Place sliced carrots in water and cook over low heat for 1 hour. Add remaining ingredients and cook until carrots are firm but tender. Serve immediately. Serves 20.

Jerry Russell
Stage West

HAWAIIAN CARROTS

2 cups fresh or frozen carrots
1 cup fresh chicken broth
¼ cup minced onion
¼ cup chopped green pepper
1 (8-ounce) can pineapple chunks,
    drained, reserving juice

2 tablespoons cornstarch
¼ cup sherry
Salt, to taste
Pepper, to taste

Place carrots and chicken broth in saucepan, cover and simmer for about 10 minutes or until carrots are nearly tender. Add onion and green pepper. Cook, uncovered, for 2 minutes. Drain liquid from saucepan. Add pineapple. Mix cornstarch with reserved pineapple juice and sherry until well-blended. Stir into simmering carrots. Cook, stirring constantly, until mixture simmers and thickens. Taste. Add salt and pepper as needed.

Ray Underwood

BAKED CORN IN SOUR CREAM

6 bacon slices
2 tablespoons chopped onion
2 tablespoons butter
2 tablespoons all-purpose flour
½ teaspoon salt

1 cup sour cream
2 (12-ounce) cans whole kernel corn,
    drained
1 tablespoon chopped parsley

Fry bacon, drain and crumble. Set aside. Sauté onion in butter, blend in flour and salt. Gradually add sour cream, stirring until mixture is smooth. Heat just to boiling, add cream and heat thoroughly. Fold in half the bacon. Spoon into a greased 2-quart casserole, top with parsley and remaining bacon. Bake at 350° for 30 to 45 minutes. Yields 6 servings.

Mrs. Margaret Lowdon

TEXAS STYLE CORN
Sacred simplicity!

1 can white corn
1 small can diced green chilies

1 (3-ounce) package cream cheese

Mix ingredients in a saucepan and stir over low heat until cheese begins to melt. Pour into a small casserole and bake at 325° for 15 to 20 minutes.

Morgan Fairchild
Actress

EGGPLANT CASSEROLE

1 medium eggplant	Salt, to taste
1 large onion	Pepper, to taste
½ stick butter or margarine, melted	2 cups cream style corn (1 can)
2 eggs, beaten	1 green pepper, diced (optional)
1 cup cracker crumbs	1 cup grated sharp Cheddar cheese

Pare eggplant, cut into 1-inch cubes and cook until tender. Chop onion and sauté in butter or margarine. Drain eggplant, mix with all ingredients except cheese and transfer to baking dish. Sprinkle cheese on top. Bake at 350° until puffed. Serves 8.

Mrs. J. Herman Musick (Celeste)

EGGPLANT PARMESAN I

2 cups tomato sauce	Oregano, to taste
1 medium eggplant	Garlic powder, to taste
1 cup seasoned Italian bread crumbs	Onion powder, to taste
8 ounces mozzarella cheese, grated	Mushrooms (optional)
Grated Parmesan cheese	Swiss cheese (optional)

Spread ¼ cup tomato sauce over bottom of baking dish. Wash eggplant and cut into ½-inch slices. Do not peel. Layer eggplant, bread crumbs, tomato sauce, mozzarella and Parmesan cheeses. Season with oregano, garlic and onion powder. Bake at 350° for 30 to 40 minutes or until eggplant is tender and cheese bubbles. Serve over pasta. A layer of sautéed mushrooms is delicious, as is a layer of Swiss cheese.

Mrs. Mickey Leland (Alison Walton)
Wife, U. S. Congressman

EGGPLANT PARMESAN II

1 eggplant
Oil or shortening
1 or 2 eggs
Milk
Prepared bread crumbs
Salt

Pepper
Garlic powder
1 (16-ounce) jar spaghetti sauce with
   mushrooms
Mozzarella cheese
Grated Parmesan cheese

Peel and slice eggplant into thick slices. Soak in cold water, then drain well. Grease a large oblong pan and set aside. Heat enough oil or shortening in a skillet to brown eggplant. In small dish, beat 1 or 2 eggs, depending on size of eggplant, and add milk, using half an egg shell to measure. (For 1 egg, use half egg shell of milk.) Dip sliced eggplant in egg mixture and then in bread crumbs. Brown both sides in skillet. After browning, put single layer in dish. Season with salt, pepper and garlic powder. Spread small amount of spaghetti sauce on each slice. Top each slice generously with mozzarella cheese. Add remaining spaghetti sauce and sprinkle well with Parmesan cheese. Bake at 350° for 15 to 20 minutes or until cheese is hot and bubbly and eggplant is tender. Serve hot.

Mrs. Tom Pollard (Carole)
Wife, Mayor of Kerrville, Texas

ESCALLOPED EGGPLANT

2 pounds eggplant
2 eggs
4 tablespoons butter
½ cup minced onion
Garlic, to taste
1 cup cracker meal

1 cup grated American cheese
½ cup milk
Salt, to taste
Pepper, to taste
1 cup grated cheese

Peel and cube eggplant. Cook until tender, drain and mash. Stir in eggs, butter, onions, garlic, cracker meal, American cheese, milk, salt and pepper. Transfer to an oiled baking dish, top with cheese and bake at 350° for 30 minutes.

Allan Shivers
Governor of Texas
1949-1957

Page 150 (representing the Texas Sesquicentennial) has been reserved for the BEST OF BOOK RECIPE.

SAUTÉED MUSHROOMS

2 tablespoons minced onion
1 stick butter or margarine
1 pound sliced fresh mushrooms
1 tablespoon garlic powder

8 ounces sour cream
1 cup rosé wine
¼ teaspoon salt
¼ teaspoon white pepper

Over medium heat cook onion in butter until tender. Add mushrooms and garlic and cook until mushrooms are tender. Add remaining ingredients and simmer over low heat for 30 minutes. Serve. Serves 4.

Jerry Russell
Stage West

VANDERGRIFF SOUTHERN OKRA

1 cup cut okra
1 medium onion, chopped
1 green pepper, chopped
¼ cup salad oil
3 tomatoes, peeled and quartered or 1
   cup canned tomatoes

1 tablespoon sugar
1 teaspoon flour
½ teaspoon salt
½ teaspoon pepper

Cook okra in boiling, salted water for 10 minutes; drain. Brown onion and green pepper in salad oil. Add tomatoes and cook slowly for 5 minutes. Stir in okra, sugar, flour, salt and pepper. Cook over low heat until vegetables are just tender, stirring as little as possible.

Mrs. Tom Vandergriff (Anna Waynette)
Wife, U. S. Congressman

POTATOES ROMANOFF

8 good-sized red potatoes
2 (10-ounce) cartons sour cream
1¾ cups grated sharp Cheddar cheese
1 bunch tiny green onions, chopped

2¾ teaspoons salt
¼ teaspoon pepper
Paprika

Boil potatoes in jackets in hot water until fork tender. Peel and shred into large bowl. Stir in sour cream, 1 cup cheese, onions, salt and pepper. Turn into buttered 2-quart casserole. Top with remaining cheese and sprinkle with paprika. Cover and refrigerate for several hours or overnight. Bake, covered, in preheated 350° oven for 30 to 40 minutes until heated through. Uncover the last 10 to 15 minutes to melt cheese.

Jan Carson
News Anchor
KPRC-TV
Houston, Texas

HOT POTATO SALAD WITH BACON
Kartoffelsalat Mit Speck

2¾ pounds boiling potatoes
½ pound bacon slices, diced
1¼ cups chopped onion
1 cup chopped green pepper
⅔ cup beef bouillon

2 tablespoons cider vinegar
1½ teaspoons salt
¼ teaspoon white pepper
1¼ teaspoons sugar
Parsley

Cook potatoes in salted water until tender; drain. Peel potatoes, cut into ½-inch slices. Fry bacon until crisp. Remove and drain on paper towels. Use ¼ cup bacon drippings to sauté onions until golden; stir in green peppers, beef bouillon, cider vinegar, salt, white pepper and sugar. Cook about 1½ minutes or until green pepper is tender-crisp. Add potatoes and bacon and toss gently until combined. Cover skillet. Cook over medium heat just until potatoes are hot. Garnish with border of parsley. Yields 8 servings.

Mrs. Al Worn (Carol)

SKILLET HOPPING JOHN

2 tablespoons margarine, melted
2 (16-ounce) cans black-eyed peas,
  drained and rinsed
2 cups chicken and vegetable bouillon

1 cup uncooked regular rice
1 teaspoon salt
Crushed red pepper
Onion salt, to taste

Mix ingredients in large skillet. Cover and simmer for 1 hour or until rice is done.

Mrs. Tom Vandergriff (Anna Waynette)
Wife, U. S. Congressman

RICE WITH PINE NUTS

3 cups beef stock (2 cans Campbell's
  diluted to make 3 cups)
1½ cups Uncle Ben's converted long
  grain white rice

8 tablespoons butter
⅓ cup pine nuts (from health food store)
⅓ cup golden raisins

Bring stock to a boil, add rice and butter. Cover and simmer for 20 minutes until liquid is absorbed. Heat the remaining butter until slightly bubbly, add the pine nuts and continue heating until browned. (This happens quickly and the nuts can easily overbrown.) Pour the nuts and butter over the rice, add raisins, fluff the mixture with a fork, then cover and let stand for 5 minutes. Note: For variation, you may use chicken broth instead of beef, and/or use pecans instead of pine nuts. Serves 6.

Mrs. Tom Loeffler (Kathy)
Wife, U. S. Congressman

BAKED RICE

¼ cup plus 2 tablespoons butter
1 cup raw rice
1 can consommé

1 small jar mushrooms with liquid
½ can onion soup

Layer all ingredients in casserole in order listed. Cover and bake at 350° for 35 minutes. Uncover and bake 10 more minutes.

Mrs. Al Worn (Carol)

TEXAS GREEN RICE

2 cups rice
1½ to 2 cups milk
½ cup salad oil
1 cup chopped green pepper

1 cup chopped parsley
1 cup chopped green onions with tops
1 to 2 garlic cloves, minced
1 pound cheese, grated

Cook rice. Combine all ingredients, reserving some cheese for topping. Mix well. Transfer to baking dish and top with reserved cheese. Bake at 350° for 1 hour. Serves 12.

Jack Brooks
U. S. Congressman

PERSIAN RICE

2 cups rice
1 heaping tablespoon butter
1 very large onion, sliced
¼ pound pine or pecan nuts, broken

½ pound seedless raisins
Cinnamon
Water

Boil rice. Heat butter and fry onion slices, nuts and raisins until raisins are puffed. Butter a baking dish and cover the bottom with onion slices. Add half the cooked rice, then all the fried ingredients. Cover with cinnamon and top with remaining rice. Make 3 holes with a tablespoon to the bottom of the dish. Pour 1 tablespoon water in each hole. Cover and bake for 5 minutes in a hot oven, then for 1 hour in a slow oven.

Mel Dacus
Katy Dacus

SPINACH DORINNE

2 packages frozen chopped spinach
4 tablespoons butter
2 tablespoons flour
2 tablespoons chopped onions
½ cup spinach liquid
½ cup evaporated milk
½ teaspoon black pepper

½ teaspoon salt
¾ teaspoon celery salt
¾ teaspoon garlic salt
1 teaspoon Worcestershire sauce
Red pepper
1 (6-ounce) roll Kraft jalapeño cheese
Seasoned bread crumbs

Cook spinach according to package directions; drain, reserving liquid. Melt butter in saucepan over low heat. Add flour and stir until smooth. Add onions and cook until soft. Add liquid of spinach and evaporated milk and cook until thick, stirring constantly. Add pepper, salt, celery salt, garlic salt, Worcestershire sauce, red pepper and cheese and stir until melted. Combine with spinach. Put in casserole and top with bread crumbs. Bake at 350° for 30 minutes. May be frozen. Serves 5 to 6.

Mrs. Mark C. Hill (Kathy)

SPANISH SQUASH

2 pounds yellow squash, sliced
1 medium onion, sliced
1 small can green chilies with juice, chopped

2 eggs, beaten
¾ cup grated sharp cheese
½ cup Miracle Whip salad dressing
¼ cup dry bread crumbs

Cook squash and onion in as little water as possible; drain. Add remaining ingredients. Bake in a greased 2-quart dish at 375° for 30 minutes. Note: I mix a few more bread crumbs and grated cheese on top the last few minutes.

Ray Underwood

SQUASH CASSEROLE

Butter
Squash (for 8 servings)
1 bunch green onions, chopped

¼ pound American cheese, grated
Lay's barbecued potato chips, crushed

Melt butter in skillet. Barely cook squash with the green onions. Add the cheese and stir until melted. Pour into casserole and top with crushed potato chips. Serves 8.

Mrs. C. Harold Brown (Carol)

AGGIELAND ZUCCHINI

5 to 6 medium zucchini, cucumber sliced
1 medium white onion, diced
2 to 3 medium tomatoes, diced

1 teaspoon garlic
1 teaspoon pepper
8 ounces mozzarella cheese, grated

Lightly brown the zucchini in a large skillet (dry, no oil) on medium heat. Add onion and brown lightly. Add tomatoes, garlic and pepper and let simmer for 10 minutes on low heat with a lid on the skillet. Pour contents of skillet into a large cooking bowl and bake at 350° for 10 minutes. Top with cheese and return to oven for 10 more minutes. Serve hot from oven.

Bob Cannon
Mama's Pizza
College Station, Texas

SCRAMBLED TOFU

2 tablespoons sesame oil
½ cup sliced fresh mushrooms
1 (8-ounce) cake of tofu
1 teaspoon Tamari soy sauce

½ teaspoon oregano
1 teaspoon parsley flakes
1 teaspoon garlic powder

Heat oil over medium heat. Sauté mushrooms until brown. Crumble in tofu and heat and stir for 2 to 3 minutes. Add remaining ingredients, reduce heat to low and cook for 8 to 10 minutes. Serve with rye toast, sliced tomatoes and alfalfa sprouts.

Jordan Gold

This photograph depicts Texas, with its bluebonnets, cactus, and barbed wire fence, framed with mesquite trees. The bluebonnet was adopted as the state flower of Texas in 1901 at the request of the Society of Colonial Dames. While it symbolizes the often fragile appearing beauty of the harsh Texas landscape, it is, in fact, a plant as hardy and resilient as the cactus and mesquite, which have managed to survive the extremes of climate which occur with regularity in Texas. Both the cactus and mesquite have, in fact, helped ranchers keep their cattle alive when all other vegetation had disappeared. The barbed wire is symbolic of converting the open range lands of Texas to the productive ranches of today.

STATE OF TEXAS

Dear Mr. Gardner:

Here is a recipe for Lemon Yogurt Cake for your cookbook. It
sounds like a good project -- good luck!

1 c. butter or margarine
2 c. sugar
6 eggs, separated
2 t. grated lemon peel
½ t. lemon extract
3 c. cake flour
1 t. soda
¼ t. salt
1 c. yogurt

Beat yogurt and 1½c. of sugar with electric mixer until creamy.
Add egg yolks, lemon peel, lemon extract and beat until thick
and pale yellow. Sift the flour, measure, and sift again with
the soda and salt. Into the creamed butter mixture alternately
mix the flour and the yogurt. Beat the egg whites until soft
peaks form; then gradually add the remaining ½ c. sugar,
beating until glossy. Fold batter into beaten egg whites and
pour into a greased 10-inch tube pan. Bake at 350° for 45
minutes or until done. Cool 15 minutes in pan, then turn out
on a rack. 12 -15 servings.

Sincerely,

Ann W. Richards

ANN W. RICHARDS
State Treasurer

AWR/mbh

BOB BOLEN
MAYOR

Chocolate Cake

1/2 cup Crisco vegetable shortening
1/2 cup cocoa
1 cup boiling water
2 cups flour
2 cups sugar
1 1/2 teaspoons soda
1/2 cup buttermilk
2 eggs, unbeaten
1 teaspoon vanilla

Mix Crisco, cocoa and boiling water; set aside to cool.
Mix flour with sugar and soda. Stir in liquid ingredients
and beat. Add butermilk, eggs and vanilla. Bake in
prepared 12 x 9 inch oblong cake pan at 350 degrees for
45 - 50 minutes.

Creamy Frosting

2 1/2 tablespoons flour
1/2 cup milk
1/2 cup shortening
1/2 cup granulated sugar
1/2 teaspoon vanilla
1/4 teaspoon salt

Blend flour into milk and cook until mixture becomes a
thick paste. Cool thoroughly. While paste is cooling,
cream shortening with sugar; add vanilla and salt. When
paste is cool, add by spoonfuls to creamed mixture and
keep beating with electric mixture until fluffy. The more
you beat the fluffier it will be.

Mrs. Bob Bolen

BILL ARCHER
7TH DISTRICT, TEXAS

MEMBER:
WAYS AND MEANS
COMMITTEE

Congress of the United States
House of Representatives
Washington, D.C. 20515

Dump Cake

Butter
1 can crushed pineapple (21 oz.)
1 can cherry pie filling (20 oz.)
1 package white or yellow cake mix
2 sticks of butter or margarine
Nuts of choice
Whipped cream or Cool-Whip

Butter the bottom of an oblong cake pan. Dump crushed
pineapple in the pan and spread evenly. Dump cherry
pie filling and spread over pineapple. Dump cake mix
right from the package over pie filling. Slice sticks of
butter or margarine into pats, and arrange evenly over
cake mix. Sprinkle nuts of your choice over mixture.
Bake at 350 degrees for approximately one hour. Serve
topped with whipped cream or Cool Whip.

Bill Archer
Member of Congress

Raspberry Riches

Raspberry Cake

- 1 cup sifted all-purpose flour
- 3/4 cup sugar
- 1/2 tsp. baking powder
- 1/4 tsp. baking soda
- 1/4 tsp. salt
- 1 egg
- 1/3 cup buttermilk
- 1/2 tsp. vanilla extract
- 1/3 cup unsalted butter, melted and cooled to room temperature
- 1 1/4 cup. fresh red raspberries
- Sugar - Crumb Topping

Preheat oven to 375°. Butter a 9" round or a 8" square baking pan.

Sift together flour, sugar, baking powder and soda, and salt into a large mixing bowl. In another bowl, beat together egg, buttermilk and vanilla until smooth. Stir in the butter. Pour liquid mixture into the flour mixture and beat with a wooden spoon until nearly smooth. Spread batter evenly in prepared pan. Sprinkle with raspberries.

FINISH WITH A LAYER OF SUGAR-CRUMB TOPPING.

BAKE UNTIL RICHLY BROWNED, ABOUT 40 TO 45 MINUTES. LET CAKE COOL ON A RACK UNTIL WARM. SERVE WARM.

MAKES 10 SERVINGS.

SUGAR - CRUMB TOPPING

½ CUP FIRMLY PACKED LIGHT BROWN SUGAR

2 TBSP. FLOUR

1 TBSP. UNSALTED BUTTER, CUT INTO SMALL PIECES.

1½ TSP. (½ OUNCE) SEMI-SWEET CHOCOLATE, FINELY GRATED

WITH METAL BLADE, ADD ALL INGREDIENTS TO BOWL OF FOOD PROCESSOR. PROCESS TO A FINE CONSISTENCY.

BLACK RUSSIAN CAKE

1 (18½-ounce) box deep chocolate cake
  mix
½ cup oil
1 (4½ ounce) package instant chocolate
  pudding

4 eggs, at room temperature
1 cup strong coffee
¼ cup coffee liqueur
¼ cup creme de cacao

Preheat oven to 350°. Blend all ingredients in large mixing bowl. Beat 3 minutes at medium speed. Bake in a greased and floured bundt pan for 45 to 55 minutes. Cool in pan for 20 minutes, then remove from pan. Punch holes in cake with meat fork. Spoon topping over cake.

TOPPING

1 cup strong coffee
1 cup confectioners' sugar, sifted

2 tablespoons coffee liqueur
2 tablespoons creme de cacao

Combine all ingredients, mixing well. Spoon over warm cake. Note: This topping is also good with ice cream.

Mrs. M. C. Newell (Helen)

BAY'S BEST CHOCOLATE CAKE

2 cups sugar
¼ teaspoon salt
⅔ cup Crisco
2 squares Baker's semisweet chocolate
2 eggs, unbeaten

3 cups flour
1 cup buttermilk
1 teaspoon soda
½ cup boiling water
1 teaspoon vanilla

Cream sugar, salt and Crisco at least 10 minutes or until mixture looks creamy. (This is important.) Melt chocolate and add to mixture. Add eggs and blend well. Alternately add flour and buttermilk. Put soda into boiling water and add to mixture. Add vanilla. Bake at 350° for 20 to 25 minutes or until the cake comes away from the sides of the pan.

FROSTING

½ stick margarine
2 squares Baker's semisweet chocolate
1 package confectioners' sugar

1 teaspoon vanilla
Evaporated milk (enough to make good
  consistency)

Melt margarine and chocolate and add to sugar. Add vanilla and enough evaporated milk to make the filling desired consistency. Spread immediately over cooled cake.

Bragg Stockton
Head Baseball Coach
Texas Christian University

TEXAS HOT COCOA CAKE

¼ pound butter (no substitute)
½ cup Mazola vegetable oil
3 tablespoons cocoa
1 cup water
2 cups sugar
2 cups quick-blending Wonder flour

½ cup buttermilk
2 eggs
1 teaspoon soda
1 teaspoon cinnamon
1 teaspoon vanilla

Melt butter with vegetable oil, cocoa and water in a saucepan. Bring to a boil and stir. Sift sugar and flour into a large bowl. Pour liquid mixture over flour mixture and beat until smooth. Add buttermilk, eggs, soda, cinnamon and vanilla, mixing well. Pour into a prepared 13x9-inch Pyrex baking dish and bake at 400° for 35 minutes. Spread the following icing over hot cake in baking pan.

ICING
¼ pound butter
2½ tablespoons cocoa
6 tablespoons milk
1 (1-pound) box confectioners' sugar

1 teaspoon vanilla
1 cup coarsely chopped pecans (not
    ground)

Melt butter, cocoa and milk in a saucepan. Do not boil. Stir in confectioners' sugar, vanilla and pecans. While icing is hot, pour over cake in baking pan as soon as cake is removed from the oven. Icing will drip into the cake and over the sides.

Mrs. F. Howard Walsh

MUD CAKE

FIRST LAYER
1 cup flour
1 stick margarine

1 cup chopped pecans

Blend flour with margarine, and then add pecans. Press into a 13x9-inch pan. Bake at 350° for 25 minutes.

SECOND LAYER
1 cup Cool Whip
1 teaspoon vanilla
1 cup confectioners' sugar

1 (8-ounce) package cream cheese, softened

Blend ingredients and pour over cool crust.

THIRD LAYER
1 teaspoon vanilla
1 small package instant vanilla or chocolate pudding mix
1¾ cups milk

1 cup Cool Whip
Chopped pecans, to garnish
Shaved chocolate (Hershey bar), to garnish

Blend vanilla, pudding mix and milk; pour over cream cheese mixture. Top with Cool Whip and sprinkle with pecans and/or shaved chocolate.

Charlie Lanier Turner
Head Basketball Coach
Paschal High School
From 1943-1973

CHEESECAKE BY ADALINE PETTA

CRUST
16 to 18 graham crackers, crushed to
   fine crumbs

4 tablespoons margarine
4 tablespoons sugar

Mix cracker crumbs with margarine and sugar.

CHEESECAKE
1 large package cream cheese
2 eggs
½ cup sugar

1 teaspoon vanilla
1 teaspoon lemon juice

Beat cream cheese until easy to mix. Add 1 egg at a time and continue to beat as you add sugar. Add vanilla and lemon juice. Butter a springform pan with melted butter. Press crumbs in bottom and sides of pan. Pour in filling mixture and bake at 350° for 30 minutes. Cool and chill. Spread with topping and serve.

TOPPING
½ pint sour cream
3 teaspoons sugar

3 teaspoons vanilla

Mix ingredients and spread over chilled cheesecake.

Mrs. Adaline Petta

GEORGE LOKEY'S FAMOUS PEACH CHEESECAKE

CRUST

1 box graham crackers (or graham
   cracker crumbs)

2 tablespoons sugar
½ pound butter, melted

Chop up graham crackers in Cuisinart if you can't find the crumbs. Mix with sugar and butter. Put in a large springform pan. I find that using a crystal glass helps form the crust on the bottom and sides of the springform pan with very little effort. After getting at least a ¼-inch crust on the sides and bottom, set the pan aside.

CHEESECAKE

5 (8-ounce) packages Philadelphia
   cream cheese (2½ pounds)
1¾ cups sugar
3 tablespoons flour
1 tablespoon fresh lime juice
2 tablespoons fresh lemon juice

1 tablespoon strong vanilla (Mexican, if
   you have it)
7 eggs
½ cup whipping cream
1 cup fresh chopped peaches (Stillwell's
   frozen, if fresh aren't available)

Get your cream cheese to room temperature. Combine cream cheese and sugar in a large mixer. Add flour, lime juice, lemon juice and vanilla; mix well. Then add 5 eggs, 1 at a time, mixing well. Then add 2 egg yolks, 1 at a time, and again mix well. Fold in whipping cream. At the last minute, put chopped fresh peaches in mixture. Pour mixture into already prepared graham cracker crumb crust in springform pan. Bake in preheated 500° oven for 10 minutes, then reduce heat to 250° and bake for 1 hour. Note: This recipe is hard to beat. It was given to me by my neighbor, Judge Hugh Russell, and I made a few minor variations myself. I understand it comes from Lindy's in New York, which is reputed to have one of the better cheesecakes. I especially put the peaches in this cheesecake so it would harmonize well with one of my favorite dessert wines. I suggest you check with your wine merchant, and have him secure for you a bottle of Robert Mondavi Muscot D-Oro. Chill wine before serving.

George Lokey
Ted Lokey Oil Company

PINEAPPLE-APPLE CAKE

1 cup flour
½ teaspoon salt
1½ cups sugar
2 eggs
2 cups diced apples

1 cup chopped pecans
2 teaspoons vanilla
½ cup drained crushed pineapple
Whipped cream, to garnish

Sift flour with salt; add sugar and eggs. Mix well. Stir in apples, pecans, vanilla and pineapple. Pour into prepared 8x8-inch pan. Bake at 350° for 30 minutes. Serve with whipped cream.

Jack C. Vowell
State Representative

MOM'S OLD-FASHIONED BANANA NUT CAKE

2¼ cups flour
1½ teaspoons baking powder
¾ teaspoon soda
¾ teaspoon salt
1½ cups sugar
¾ cup shortening
½ cup brown sugar

2 cups mashed bananas
6 tablespoons buttermilk
3 eggs
1½ teaspoons vanilla
¾ cup chopped pecans, dusted with 6
  tablespoons flour

Mix flour, baking powder, soda, salt and granulated sugar. Add shortening, brown sugar, bananas and milk; mix. Add eggs, vanilla and nuts; mix well. Bake in 3 regular cake pans at 375° for 30 minutes or until done. Ice with your favorite icing.

Ann Owens Gilliland
Journalist

PECAN CAKE

1 pound butter or margarine
1 pound sugar (2 cups)
6 eggs
1½ ounces lemon extract
¾ ounce water

1 pound flour (4 cups)
1½ teaspoons baking powder
1 pound white raisins
1 pound pecans (2 cups)

Cream butter and sugar; add eggs, lemon extract and water. Add flour and baking powder, mixing well. Stir in raisins and pecans. Bake in a prepared tube pan or 2 loaf pans at 250° to 275° for 1½ hours.

Jack C. Vowell
State Representative

COCONUT REFRIGERATOR CAKE

1 box butter recipe cake mix
1½ cups sugar
1 (6-ounce) carton sour cream

1 (12-ounce) package frozen coconut, thawed
1 (8-ounce) carton Cool Whip

Prepare cake mix according to package directions, making 2 (9-inch) round layers. When cool, split both layers. Combine sugar, sour cream and coconut, blending well. Chill. Reserve 1 cup of mixture for frosting. Spread remainder between layers of cake, split side up. Combine reserved sour cream mixture with Cool Whip and blend. Spread on top and sides of cake. Seal in airtight container and refrigerate for 3 days. It is good after 1 day if you can't wait. May be frozen.

Mrs. Ron Paul (Carol)
Wife, U. S. Congressman

AUNT DOROTHY'S ITALIAN CREAM CAKE

1 stick butter
½ cup Crisco
2 cups sugar
5 egg yolks, beaten
2 cups flour

1 teaspoon soda
1 cup buttermilk
1 teaspoon vanilla
1 cup coconut
5 egg whites, beaten

Cream butter and Crisco. Add sugar and beat until smooth. Add beaten egg yolks. Combine flour and soda and add to mixture alternately with buttermilk. Stir in vanilla and coconut. Fold in egg whites. Put into 3 greased and floured cake pans. Bake at 350° for 25 minutes.

Charles Mayberry

SOUR CREAM PLAIN CAKE

1 cup butter or margarine (½ pound)
2¾ cups sugar
6 eggs
3 cups flour
½ teaspoon salt

¼ teaspoon soda
1 (8-ounce) carton sour cream
½ teaspoon vanilla
½ teaspoon lemon extract
1 teaspoon orange flavoring

Mix butter and sugar until light and fluffy. Add eggs, 1 at a time, beating well. Sift flour with salt and soda. Add alternately with sour cream, starting and ending with flour. Beat well. Add flavorings. Bake in a prepared tube pan at 300° for 1½ hours.

Mrs. Sam Jackson (Faye)

1-2-3-4 CAKE

1 cup butter
2 cups sugar
4 eggs
3 cups flour

3 teaspoons baking powder
1 cup milk
1 teaspoon vanilla

Cream butter and sugar thoroughly. Add eggs, 1 at a time. Sift flour twice then measure. Add baking powder and resift. Add flour and milk alternately to first mixture. Stir in vanilla and bake in prepared large loaf pan at 375° until done.

Mrs. William R. Gardner (Mary Ann)

PINEAPPLE FLOP CAKE

2 cups flour
2 teaspoons soda

1½ cups sugar
1 large can crushed pineapple

Mix flour, soda and sugar. Stir in pineapple. Pour into a greased, floured pan and bake at 350° until cake tests done.

ICING
1 small can evaporated milk
1 stick margarine

1 cup sugar

Mix milk, margarine and sugar in a saucepan. Bring to a boil and cook, stirring constantly, for 4 minutes. Remove from heat and stir in pecans, coconut and vanilla. Pour over hot cake.

Mrs. Sam Jackson (Faye)

PUMPKIN CAKE
Great for Thanksgiving dinner.

4 eggs, well-beaten
2 cups sugar
1 cup salad oil
2 cups flour

2 teaspoons soda
2 teaspoons cinnamon
½ teaspoon salt
1 can pumpkin

Mix eggs, sugar and oil in a large bowl. Sift flour, soda, cinnamon and salt, and add to egg mixture. Mix well and add pumpkin. Pour into a prepared bundt pan and bake at 350° for about 1 hour or until well done. Cool and spread with icing.

ICING
1 (8-ounce) package cream cheese
½ stick margarine
1 box confectioners' sugar

1 cup chopped pecans
1 teaspoon vanilla

Mix well and spread on cooled cake.

Mrs. R. P. Klein (Mary Beth)
Wife, Mayor of Amarillo, Texas

14 "CAROT" CAKE

2 cups flour
1½ teaspoons soda
2 teaspoons baking powder
1 teaspoon salt
2 teaspoons cinnamon
2 cups sugar

1½ cups oil
4 eggs
2 cups grated carrots
1 (8¾-ounce) can crushed pineapple,
  drained
½ cup chopped nuts

Sift flour, soda, baking powder, salt and cinnamon. Add sugar, oil and eggs. Mix well. Add carrots, pineapple and nuts. Blend. Turn into 3 greased and floured 9-inch layer pans. Bake at 350° for 35 to 40 minutes. Cool a few minutes in pans, then turn out and cool on wire racks. Fill layers and spread top and sides with frosting. Cake will be very brown as it bakes.

CREAM CHEESE FROSTING
½ cup butter, softened
1 (8-ounce) package cream cheese,
  softened

1 teaspoon vanilla
1 pound confectioners' sugar
Milk (optional)

Mix butter, cream cheese and vanilla. Cream well. Add sugar gradually. Beat well. If too thick, add small amount of milk to thin.

Johnny Rutherford
Professional Race Car Driver

PINEAPPLE ANGEL CAKE

1 pint whipping cream
1 package instant vanilla pudding mix
1 large can crushed pineapple

1 teaspoon vanilla
Sugar, to taste
1 angel food cake

Whip cream, stir in pudding mix, add pineapple and vanilla. Blend in sugar. Split cake horizontally. Spread filling between layers, on sides and top of cake, using all filling. Refrigerate. Serves 12.

Mrs. Tom Pollard (Carole)
Wife, Mayor of Kerrville, Texas

STRAWBERRY ANGEL CAKE

1 (3-ounce) package strawberry gelatin
1 cup boiling water
1 (12-ounce) package frozen
   strawberries, thawed
1 cup heavy cream, whipped

1 angel food cake
Additional whipped cream, to garnish
Whole fresh strawberries, to garnish

Dissolve gelatin in boiling water. Stir in thawed strawberries. Chill until partially set. Fold in whipped cream and chill until firm. Slice angel food cake into 2 layers. Spread strawberry cream mixture between layers and on top of cake. Additional whipped cream may be spread on sides and top of cake. Decorate with whole strawberries. Refrigerate cake for several hours or overnight before serving.

Ben H. Procter

COCONUT POUND CAKE

1 cup butter, softened
2 cups sugar
3 eggs
3 cups all-purpose flour, sifted
2 teaspoons baking powder

¼ teaspoon salt
½ teaspoon lemon extract
½ teaspoon vanilla
1 cup milk
1 cup flaked coconut

Cream butter with sugar. Add eggs, 1 at a time, beating well after each addition. Sift flour with baking powder and salt. Add lemon extract and vanilla to milk. Add flour mixture alternately with milk mixture to creamed butter and sugar. Mix well. Stir in coconut. Pour into greased and floured 10-inch tube pan. Bake at 350° for about 55 minutes or until cake tests done. Cool 10 minutes in pan, then remove from pan and cool on rack. Yields 16 to 20 slices.

Mrs. J. Herman Musick (Celeste)

Mary Martin

Pecan Pie —

3 eggs, beaten
3/4 cup of sugar
3/4 cup " white Karo
3 Tabs. melted butter
1 teas. white vinegar
1 teas. vanilla
1 cup pecans, chopped
1/8 tea. salt. ———

Thoroughly mix all ingredients except pecans. Add pecans and mix. Pour mixture into a unbaked pie shell. Bake in preheated 375° oven for 25-30 min. until knife or fork — used to prick center comes clean. — Mary Martin

173

TOWN OF **South Padre Island**

Dear Russell:

I feel very honored to have been asked to join such
an illustrious group making contributions to your
cookbook.

Enclosed you will find my recipe for my favorite
lemon pie and I hope that your readers will find
it equally delightful.

I wish you much success in your endeavor and I shall
be proud to receive a copy of the finished product.

Sincerely,

Minnie Solomonson
Mayor

MS/dmm
Enclosure

ELEGANT/DELICATE LEMON MERINGUE PIE

7 Eggs, separated
1 Full Cup of Sugar
2 Lemons - juice and rind
1 Baked pie crust

Beat yolks until lemon color, add sugar, juice and
rind. Cook in double boiler until thick like
custard.

Cool yolk mixture - whip egg whites until very
stiff. Gently fold 2/3 whites into yolk mixture. Pour into baked crust

Beat remaining whites again with 2 Tablespoons
sugar per egg (about 6 Tablespoons), adding
gradually to make a stiff meringue. Spread on
pie crust and bake in a slow oven, 300 to 325,
until brown on top.

                    Minnie Solomonson
                    Mayor

BOB BOLEN
MAYOR

Strawberry Ice Box Pie

1/2 cup granulated sugar
1 envelope unflavored gelatin
1/2 cup water
1 10 oz. pkg. frozen sliced strawberries
juice of 1/2 lemon
1/8 teaspoon vanilla
1 cup heavy cream - whipped

In saucepan, stir sugar with gelatin. Stir in water, then
cook over low heat, stirring until just below boiling point.
Remove from heat. Add unthawed strawberries, lemon
juice and vanilla. Stir, breaking up berries with fork,
until berries thaw. Mixture will thicken. Then fold in
whipped cream. Pour filling into baked crust. Refrigerat
for about one hour or until set.

Mrs. Bob Bolen

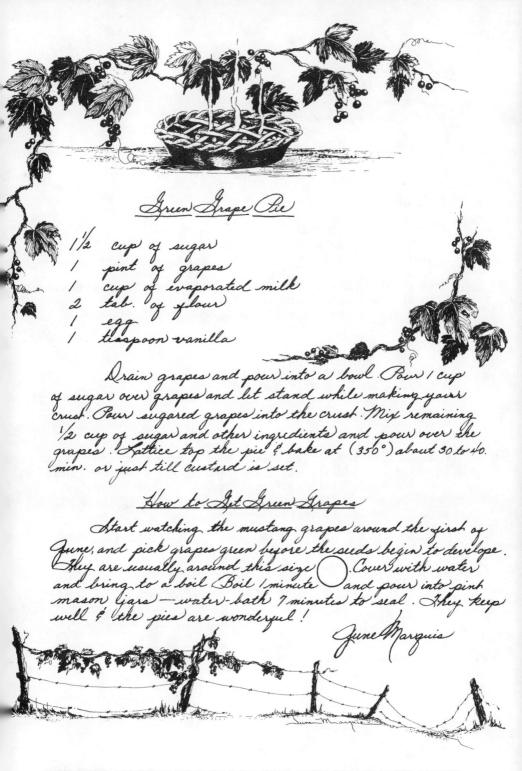

Green Grape Pie

1½ cup of sugar
1   pint of grapes
1   cup of evaporated milk
2   tab. of flour
1   egg
1   teaspoon vanilla

Drain grapes and pour into a bowl. Pour 1 cup of sugar over grapes and let stand while making your crust. Pour sugared grapes into the crust. Mix remaining ½ cup of sugar and other ingredients and pour over the grapes. Lattice top the pie & bake at (350°) about 30 to 40. min. or just till custard is set.

How to Get Green Grapes

Start watching the mustang grapes around the first of June, and pick grapes green before the seeds begin to develope. They are usually around this size ◯. Cover with water and bring to a boil Boil 1 minute and pour into pint mason jars — water-bath 7 minutes to seal. They keep well & the pies are wonderful!

June Marquis

EDITOR'S NOTE: THE SIZE OF THE GRAPE ABOVE IS NOT ACTUAL SIZE. THE LETTER HAS BEEN REDUCED TO FIT ON THE PAGE.

OREO COOKIE PIE

36 Oreo cookies, crushed
1/2 cup melted oleo
2 quarts vanilla ice cream

Make crust of Oreo cookies and oleo. Spread in oblong cake pan.
Let ice cream soften and spread over crust.
Put in freezer for several hours.

Topping:

1-1/3 cups evaporated milk
3 squares unsweetened chocolate
1/2 cup oleo
1-1/3 cups sugar
3 tsp. vanilla

Melt chocolate over low heat. Remove from heat and stir in suga
and oleo. Gradually add evaporated milk. Blend well, cook aga
over low heat, stirring frequently, until thick. Add vanilla.
Cool. Pour over ice cream and oleo mixture. Sprinkle with chop
pecans. Return to freezer and freeze again.

B. Don Magness
Chairman of the Board/ Miss Texas Pageant

HUNTING CAMP APPLE PIE

1 pie pan of thin-sliced apples
1 cup sugar
Cinnamon

1 cup flour
½ cup butter
½ cup brown sugar

Arrange apples in pie pan. Sprinkle with sugar, then with cinnamon. In a separate bowl, mix thoroughly the flour, butter and brown sugar. Pour over apples. Bake in moderate oven until apples are done.

Kelton S. Tilley (Leora)
Taxidermist

CANTALOUPE PIE

1 large cantaloupe (Pecos preferred)
Pastry for 2 (9-inch) pie crusts, unbaked
¾ cup sugar

¼ cup flour
Nutmeg
Butter

Peel and slice cantaloupe lengthwise ¼-inch thick. Layer slices all around unbaked pie shell. Mix sugar and flour and spread over cantaloupe. Sprinkle with nutmeg and dot with butter. Cover with top pastry. Bake at 450° for 10 minutes, reduce heat to 350° and bake for about 30 minutes or until golden brown.

Mrs. James E. Wright
Wife of Judge, Tarrant County, Texas

EASY PEACH COBBLER

½ to 1 stick butter
1 (1-pound) can sliced peaches
2 cups Bisquick

1 cup sugar
1 cup milk

Melt butter in a 13x9-inch dish. Pour in peaches. Mix Bisquick, sugar and milk together and pour over peaches. Bake at 375° until golden brown.

Mike Moncrief
Tarrant County Judge

BLUEBERRY-BANANA PIE

1 (8-ounce) package cream cheese,
  softened
1 cup sugar
2 envelopes Dream Whip, prepared
  according to directions

Bananas, sliced
2 pie crusts, baked
1 can blueberry pie filling, chilled

Blend cream cheese with sugar. Mix with prepared Dream Whip. Arrange banana slices over bottoms of pie crusts. Divide Dream Whip mixture between the 2 pies and spread evenly; refrigerate. Spread the chilled blueberry pie filling over the two pies. Note: Graham cracker crust may be used.

Mrs. Tom Parrett (Marcia)
Wife of Mayor, San Angelo, Texas

BUTTERMILK PIE

1 tablespoon cornstarch
1½ cups sugar
½ stick butter (no substitute)
3 eggs

1 cup buttermilk
1 teaspoon vanilla
1 frozen pie crust, thawed

Stir cornstarch into sugar. Cream with butter. Beat eggs just enough to mix. Add eggs, then buttermilk, then vanilla. Pour into crust and bake at 450° for 10 minutes. Reduce heat to 325° and continue baking for 25 to 30 minutes.

Mrs. Al Salley (Shirley)

TESSIE B'S BUTTERMILK PIE

6 tablespoons flour
3 cups sugar
6 eggs, lightly beaten
1½ cups buttermilk

1 stick margarine, melted
1 teaspoon vanilla
1 teaspoon lemon extract
2 (9-inch) pie crusts, unbaked

Mix flour with sugar. Combine eggs, buttermilk, margarine, vanilla and lemon extract; mix well. Pour into pie crusts and bake at 450° for 10 minutes, reduce heat to 325° and bake until firm.

Mrs. Susan C. Taylor
Daughter of Mayor, Dallas, Texas

SOUTHERN CHOCOLATE PIE

3 eggs, separated
Pinch of salt
1 cup sugar
2 tablespoons cornstarch
2 level tablespoons cocoa

2 cups milk
Lump of butter
1 teaspoon vanilla
1 pie crust, baked
3 tablespoons sugar

Cream egg yolks, salt and 1 cup sugar. Add cornstarch and cocoa; cream all together well. Add milk. Cook slowly, stirring constantly, until thick. Add butter and vanilla. Pour into baked pie shell. Whip egg whites with 3 tablespoons sugar until stiff. Spread this meringue over pie and heat at 320° until brown.

Dawn Queen McDavid
Bill McDavid Pontiac Honda

CHOCOLATE PIE
This is Beryl's mother's recipe.

⅓ cup flour
¾ cup sugar
¼ teaspoon salt
3 tablespoons cocoa
1 cup water
1 cup milk

3 eggs, separated
1 teaspoon vanilla
1 tablespoon butter
1 pie crust, baked
Sugar, to taste (for meringue)

Thoroughly mix flour, ¾ cup sugar, salt and cocoa in a heavy saucepan. Gradually stir in water, and then add milk. When smooth, add lightly beaten egg yolks. Cook until mixture thickens, stirring vigorously. Cool, stir in vanilla and butter and pour into prebaked pie shell. Make meringue with the 3 egg whites and sweeten to taste. Top pie with meringue and heat in oven until lightly browned.

J. J. Pickle (Beryl)
U. S. Congressman

LEMON PIE

1¼ cups sugar
5 tablespoons cornstarch
2 tablespoons butter
2 cups milk
4 eggs, separated

½ cup lemon juice
Grated lemon peel
1 pie crust, baked
Sugar, to taste (for meringue)

Mix sugar with cornstarch. Mix in butter and milk; cook until thick, stirring for 6 minutes. Mix in beaten egg yolks, lemon juice and lemon peel. Pour into baked pie crust. Beat egg whites, sweeten with sugar and spread over pie. Bake until brown.

Mrs. Sam Jackson (Faye)

CREAM PECAN PIE
Menard County Pecan Show Grand Champion 1976.

2 cups sugar
1 cup water
3 tablespoons butter
4 eggs, separated
4 tablespoons cornstarch or flour

1 cup heavy cream
1½ cups chopped pecans
1 teaspoon vanilla
1 pie crust, baked
8 tablespoons sugar

Boil 2 cups sugar and the water to a thick syrup. Add butter. In a separate bowl, mix the egg yolks, cornstarch or flour and cream; add to the syrup and boil until it thickens. Stir in pecans and vanilla. Pour into a baked pie crust. Beat egg whites until soft peaks form. Add 8 tablespoons sugar and beat until stiff. Spread meringue over the pie. Brown in a 350° oven.

Mrs. Madeline Russell
Walter Russell Ranch

ORANGE PECAN PIE

1 cup light corn syrup
¼ cup sugar
¼ cup butter, melted
3 eggs, beaten
1 tablespoon flour
½ teaspoon salt

Several drops vanilla
1 tablespoon Texas orange juice
1 tablespoon grated Texas orange rind
1 cup chopped Texas pecans
1 (9-inch) pie crust, unbaked

Combine all ingredients except crust in a medium bowl; mix well. Pour into pie crust. Bake at 350° for 45 minutes. Makes 8 to 10 servings. May be frozen.

E. "Kika" de la Garza
U. S. Congressman

TEXAS PECAN PIE

4 eggs
1 cup sugar
1 cup dark corn syrup
1 cup pecans

1 teaspoon vanilla
¼ teaspoon salt
1 (9-inch) pie shell, unbaked

Beat eggs and sugar until thick. Add syrup, pecans, vanilla and salt. Pour into pie crust and bake at 300° for 1 hour or until firm.

Pitser H. Garrison
Mayor, Lufkin, Texas

PECAN PIE

1 cup sugar
1 tablespoon butter
½ teaspoon salt
3 eggs

½ cup white corn syrup
1 teaspoon vanilla
1 cup chopped pecans
1 pie crust, unbaked

Cream sugar, butter and salt until fluffy. Add eggs and mix well. Add corn syrup and vanilla and mix well. Place pecans in pie shell. Pour egg-sugar mixture over pecans. Bake at 375° for 40 to 50 minutes, or until filling is set.

Dixon Holman
Arlington City Councilman
Former Justice, Texas Court of Appeals
Former Texas Legislator
Southwest Conference Referee

GRACE'S PUMPKIN PIE

4 eggs, beaten
1 cup sugar
2 teaspoons flour
1 teaspoon cinnamon
½ teaspoon salt

1 teaspoon vanilla
2 cups canned pumpkin (1 can)
2 cups milk
2 pie crusts, unbaked

Add and stir as you go all ingredients except pie crusts. Mixture will be thin but will thicken with cooking. Pour into 2 pie crusts and cover crust edges with foil. Bake at 500° for 10 minutes, then remove foil, reduce heat to 350° and continue baking for 35 minutes or until center is set.

Dr. Bragg Stockton
Head Baseball Coach
Texas Christian University

FROZEN PUMPKIN PIE

1 cup cooked or canned pumpkin
1¼ cups sugar
½ teaspoon salt
½ teaspoon ginger

¼ teaspoon nutmeg
1 cup whipping cream, whipped
1 pint vanilla ice cream, softened
1 (9-inch) pie crust, baked and cooled

Mix pumpkin, sugar, salt, ginger and nutmeg. Fold into whipped cream. Spoon ice cream into baked pie shell. Top with pumpkin cream mixture. Freeze at least 2 hours. Makes 6 servings.

Mrs. Ron Paul (Carol)
Wife of U. S. Congressman

STRAWBERRY BANANA PIE

1 (10-ounce) package frozen sweetened
   strawberries
Water
½ cup sugar
2 tablespoons cornstarch
Juice of 1 large lemon
1 tablespoon unflavored gelatin

2 tablespoons cold water
1 (9-inch) pie crust, baked
2 or 3 bananas
½ pint whipping cream
1 tablespoon sugar
Few drops vanilla

Thaw strawberries and drain off juice. Measure juice and add enough water to make 1 cup. Blend ½ cup sugar with the cornstarch and add strawberry juice. Bring to a boil over medium heat, stirring constantly, and cook for about 3 minutes. Remove from heat and add lemon juice and gelatin which has been softened in the 2 tablespoons cold water. Let cool. Add strawberries and chill in refrigerator until slightly thickened. Spread half the strawberry mixture in the baked pie crust. Add sliced bananas. Top with remaining strawberry mixture. Chill until firm. Whip the whipping cream and fold in 1 tablespoon sugar and the vanilla. Pile lightly on pie.

PIE CRUST
1½ cups flour
½ teaspoon salt

½ cup Crisco
3 to 4 tablespoons ice water

Sift together the flour and salt. Cut in Crisco. Mix in water, a little at a time. Roll out on dough board and fit in pie pan. Bake at 375° for about 15 to 20 minutes or until lightly browned.

Mrs. Frank Rowland (Lorene)

RITZ CRACKER PIE

3 egg whites
1 cup sugar
22 Ritz crackers, crumbled
1 teaspoon vanilla

½ cup chopped pecans
Whipped cream
Grated chocolate (bitter or German)

Beat egg whites until stiff. Add sugar slowly. Add crackers, vanilla and pecans and transfer to a buttered pie pan as you would a crust. Bake at 300° for 25 minutes. When cool, fill with whipped cream and top with grated chocolate. Refrigerate for at least 6 hours.

Mrs. Robert R. Chilton

COMMITTEES:
CHAIRMAN
NATURAL RESOURCE
MEMBER
ENERGY RESOURCES

HOUSE OF REPRESENTATIVES

AUSTIN

Dear Russell,

Thank you for your letter dated March 13, 1984. I am enclosing a favorite recipe of mine for your book.

If I can be of further service, please call.

Sincerely,

Tom Craddick

TC:aw

TOM CRADDICK   **HOUSE OF REPRESENTATIVES**

AUSTIN

COMMITTEES:
CHAIRMAN
NATURAL RESOURCES
MEMBER
ENERGY RESOURCES

Tom's Chocolate Brownies

1 1/2 cups flour
1/2 teaspoon salt
1 cup margarine
6 heaping tablespoons cocoa
4 eggs
2 cups sugar
2 teaspoons vanilla
6 tablespoons margarine
1 (1 - pound) box confectioners' sugar
1/3 cup milk

Mix flour and salt. Melt 1 cup margarine in saucepan over
low heat. Blend in 3 tablespoons cocoa. Beat eggs until
light; beat in sugar gradually. Stir in cocoa mixture and flour
mixture. Add vanilla and mix well. Turn batter into a
greased 13 x 9 inch pan. Bake at 350 degrees for 35 - 40
minutes or until done. Cool. Soften 6 tablespoons margarine,
blend in confectioners' sugar, remaining cocoa and the milk.
Frost brownies with this mixture.

Tom Craddick

City of Galveston

Office of the Mayor

FAVORITE RECIPES
OF
MAYOR E. "GUS" MANUEL
GALVESTON, TEXAS

CINNAMON ICE BOX COOKIES

2 cups oleo   7 cups all-purpose flour
2 cups brown sugar   2 tsps. baking soda
2 cups white sugar   1½ tbls cinnamon (if recipe
4 eggs   doubled, use only 2 tbsps.)
                4 cups chopped pecans

Cook at 350 deg.

Cream oleo and sugar. Add eggs and mix well. Sift flour and
dry ingredients and add to mixture along with nuts.

Dough should be very stiff. Flour and roll into small rolls the
width of a cookie sheet (looks like a long cigar). Wrap each
roll in wax paper and put in pan in freezer 'til ready to bake.
(slices better when frozen).   Slice thinly and bake at 350 deg.
until a light brown - approximate 8 - 10 minutes.

These cookies may be kept in freezer for 6 months before baking.

THE ASSOCIATION OF FORMER STUDENTS

WHOLE WHEAT CHOCOLATE CHIP COOKIES

1	Cup Crisco	1	teaspoon baking soda
1½	Cups packed brown sugar	½	teaspoon salt
2	Eggs	2	Cups chopped pecans
1	teaspoon vanilla	1	Cup (6 ounces) Hershey's
2¼	Cups whole wheat flour (sift 3 times, then measure)		semisweet chocolate chips

Cream Crisco, brown sugar, eggs and vanilla. Sift flour several times; then sift together with baking soda and salt. Add to creamed mixture. Stir in pecans and chocolate chips. Drop by large rounded teaspoonsful onto ungreased cookie sheet. Bake at 375° approximately 8 to 10 minutes, until light brown.

PECAN PIE
"Surprise" BARS

- 1 Yellow Cake Mix
- ½ cup Brown Sugar
- 1½ cups dark corn syrup
- 1 teaspoon vanilla
- 4 eggs
- ½ cup butter
- 1 cup pecans

Easy Directions

Mix (1 to 2 minutes on high heat); ⅔ cup yellow cake mix, brown sugar, corn syrup vanilla, and 3 eggs. Set aside. Now mix rest of cake mix butter and the last egg. Mix till it becomes a crumbly dough & press into greased 9 x 13 pan. Bake at 350°F for 15-20 minutes until golden brown. Pour 1st mix over baked crust. Sprinkle with pecans and bake 30-35 minutes. Makes 36 RICH delicious pecan bars.

James R. Spurlock

BARBARA'S CHOCOLATE CHIP COOKIES

1 cup shortening
1 cup butter
2 cups sugar
2 cups brown sugar
4 eggs, lightly beaten
5 teaspoons vanilla
3 cups flour

2 teaspoons soda
1 teaspoon salt
6 cups oats (that cook in 1 minute)
2 (12-ounce) packages chocolate chips
1 (12-ounce) package peanut butter
  chips

Cream shortening and butter, add sugars gradually and mix well. Add eggs and vanilla. Stir flour, soda and salt together and add to the creamed mixture. Stir until mixed. Add oats and mix well. Stir in the chocolate and peanut butter chips. Drop walnut-sized cookies off a spoon onto a lightly greased baking sheet. Bake at 375° for about 10 to 12 minutes or until golden brown. *Do not overbake.* Makes 8 dozen Texas-size cookies. Note: This recipe makes a large amount. Use a 13-quart mixing bowl or cut the recipe in half.

Mrs. Barbara Gregory

CHOCOLATE CHIP COOKIES
They're great!

1 cup plus 2 tablespoons all-purpose
  flour
½ teaspoon soda
½ cup butter, softened
6 tablespoons sugar
6 tablespoons firmly packed brown
  sugar

½ teaspoon vanilla
1 egg
1 (6-ounce) package Nestle's semisweet
  chocolate morsels (1 cup)
½ cup chopped pecans

Preheat oven to 375°. In a small bowl, combine flour and soda; set aside. In a large bowl, combine butter, sugars and vanilla; beat until creamy. Beat in egg. Gradually add flour mixture; mix well. Stir in chocolate morsels and nuts. Drop by rounded measuring teaspoonfuls onto ungreased baking sheets. Bake for 8 to 10 minutes. Makes 30 cookies.

Jordan Scott

COWBOY COOKIES

1 cup shortening	½ teaspoon salt
1 cup sugar	2 cups rolled oats
1 cup brown sugar	1 teaspoon vanilla
2 eggs	1 cup raisins
2 cups flour, sifted	1 cup pecans
½ teaspoon baking powder	1 cup coconut
1 teaspoon soda	1 (6-ounce) package chocolate chips

Blend shortening and sugars. Beat in eggs. Stir in flour, baking powder, soda and salt. Stir in oats, vanilla, raisins, pecans, coconut and chocolate chips. Mix well. Drop onto greased baking sheet and bake at 350° for 15 minutes. Makes about 60 cookies.

W. T. Johnson
Hamlin National Bank
Hamlin, Texas

OATMEAL TOLL HOUSE

1½ cups flour	2 egg, unbeaten
1 teaspoon salt	1 teaspoon hot water
1 teaspoon soda	1 teaspoon vanilla
1 cup shortening	12 ounces chocolate chips
¾ cup brown sugar	2 cups quick oatmeal, uncooked
¾ cup sugar	1 cup pecans

Mix flour, salt and soda and set aside. Cream shortening, brown sugar, sugar and eggs. Stir in water and vanilla. Mix in dry ingredients. Stir in chocolate chips, oats and pecans. Drop by teaspoon onto ungreased baking sheet. Bake at 350° for 8 to 12 minutes. Yields 150 cookies.

Edmund Kuempel
State Representative

CHEWY OATMEAL COOKIES

1 cup flour
¾ teaspoon soda
½ teaspoon salt
1 teaspoon cinnamon
¼ teaspoon nutmeg
¾ cup margarine, softened

1¼ cups firmly packed brown sugar
2 eggs
1 teaspoon vanilla
2 cups uncooked oats
1 cup raisins
1 cup pecans

Sift flour, soda, salt, cinnamon and nutmeg into bowl. Add margarine, brown sugar, eggs and vanilla, beating until smooth. Stir in oats, raisins and nuts. Drop by heaping teaspoonful onto greased baking sheet. Bake at 350° for 12 to 15 minutes. Cool before storing.

Jane Jayroe
KXAS-TV
Fort Worth/Dallas
* Jane Jayroe has since moved to Oklahoma.

CAMPAIGN BROWNIES

2 sticks margarine
4 squares unsweetened chocolate
2 cups sugar
4 eggs, well-beaten

1 cup chopped pecans
1 cup flour
2 teaspoons vanilla
Confectioners' sugar

Melt margarine with chocolate. Cool. Mix in sugar, eggs, pecans, flour and vanilla. Grease and flour a 13x9-inch pan. Pour in batter and bake at 350° for 20 minutes. Remove from oven, sprinkle with confectioners' sugar and cool in pan. When cool, cut in squares.

Mrs. J. E. "Buster" Brown (Jill Ann)
Wife, State Senator

Aunt Mary Ann McColpin's Strawberry Shortcake

Pastry

4 cups all-purpose flour
2 teaspoons salt
1 1/3 cups shortening, chilled
4 tablespoons butter, chilled
8 tablespoons ice water
2 teaspoons sugar

Sift flour and salt together into mixing bowl. Combine shortening with butter and cut into flour mixture with a pastry blender. Work it until it has the grain of coarse cornmeal. Sprinkle the dough with water and toss lightly using a fork. If needed to hold the ingredients together, add 1 teaspoon to 1 tablespoon water. Form dough into 2 balls; wrap with waxed paper and refrigerate for at least 2 hours. Roll dough out on a lightly floured board to 1/8 inch thickness. Cut 10 (3-inch) rounds out of each ball. Place rounds on cookie sheet, sprinkle with sugar and prick entire surface of each round with a fork. Bake at 400 degrees for 12 minutes or until lightly browned. Cool on rack.

Fruit Glaze

1/2 pint strawberries
1/2 cup sugar
1 cup water
1 tablespoon arrowroot
1 tablespoon cold water
1 teaspoon lemon zest
1 tablespoon kirsch

Hull berries. Combine with sugar and water in a saucepan. Bring mixture to a boil, simmer for 5 minutes, and then strain. Return to saucepan and bring to a boil. Stir in arrowroot that has been disolved in cold water. Remove mixture from heat. Stir in lemon zest and kirsch. Cool before using.

Fresh Fruit

2 pints strawberries

Remove stems and cut berries into halves.   These are to be
used in assembling the shortcake.

Whipped Cream Topping

1 pint whipping cream
2 tablespoons confectioners' sugar

Combine whipping cream and sugar and beat until stiff.

Assembling the shortcake

Fresh mint sprigs, to garnish

Line 10 pastry rounds with 1 layer of strawberries.   Drizzle
with glaze.   On the bottom side of second set of pastry rounds,
spread a 1/8 - inch layer of whipped cream.   Place second
pastry round, cream side down, over strawberries.   Repeat
procedure in step 1.   Garnish top of each shortcake with
remaining whipped cream and a sprig of fresh mint.   Serves 10.

Note: I have described my aunt's recipe to Mansion Chef
Larry Adams.   This is Mr. Adams interpretation and is
the one that is prepared at the Governor's Mansion.

FOSSIL RIM

Fossil Rim Wildlife Ranch, Glen Rose, Texas, dedicated to the preservation of endangered species, is happy to share the recipe for our most requested dessert . . . Coconut Delight.

Served at the Overlook Restaurant atop the rim overlooking herds of zebra, ostrich, giraffe, etc., the dessert serves as a fitting compliment to viewing hundreds of exotic animals from a 1200' rim rock. Although hundreds of exotic animals roam freely on this 1500 acre preserve, Fossil Rim is most noted for its dedication to the preservation of rare and endangered species. Most notable being the Grevys Zebra, Scimitar-Horned Oryx, Addax and most recently the Black Rhino.

Working with the major U.S. zoos, Game Coin International, African Fund for Endangered Wildlife and others, this collective effort is a step toward assuring a balanced gene pool as well as an assured breeding collection for future generations to enjoy.

Open to the public daily, year round. Looking forward to a visit from you.

Tom Mantzel

COCONUT DELIGHT

Layer #1: 1 cup pecans, chopped
1 cup flour
1 stick (1/4 lb.) oleo
Mix and press into a 9"x13" dish. Bake at 250° for 25 minutes. Cool.

Layer #2: 11 oz. cream cheese
1/2 teaspoon vanilla
1 cup powdered sugar
1 cup Cool Whip
Mix and spread evenly over Layer #1.

Layer #3: 2 pkg. Instant Coconut Cream Pudding *
       (use only 3 cups milk)
1 teaspoon vanilla
Mix and when thick, spread over Layer #2.

Layer #4: Cool Whip
1 can Angel Flake Coconut
Toasted Pecans
Top with the above and chill.

* Optional: 1/2 cup coconut to pudding mix.

Dear Mr. Gardner:

Thank you for your letter of August 26, 1983, requesting one of my favorite recipes. The recipe below is one I like best.

Never -Fail Peanut Brittle

3 cups sugar
1 1/3 cups White corn syrup
1/2 cup water
4 cups raw peanuts
1 tablespoon butter
1 teaspoon vanilla
2 1/2 teaspoon soda

Cook together sugar, syrup and water until a thread spins or temperature reaches 250 degrees. Add peanuts, stir constantly until temperature reaches 300 degrees. Remove from heat and quickly stir in remaining ingredients. Mix well and pour onto two buttered cookie sheets. Spread as thin as possible. When cool, break into pieces and store in air-tight container in a cool dry place. Makes three pounds.

I look forward to receiving my copy of your interesting cookbook.

Please feel free to call on me any time I may be of service to you.

Sincerely,

Glenn H. Kothmann

THE FORT WORTH
ART MUSEUM

Office of the Director

Dear Mr. Farkas:

Robert Motherwell, the Abstract Expressionist painter, and his wife, Renate Ponsold, the famous photographer, are very close friends. Our families visit every summer on Cape Cod in Massachusetts, and as Bob and I have back-to-back birthdays in late January, we celebrate the occasion on Super Bowl Sunday, at their house and studios in Greenwic Connecticut. A classic French country meal is dinner, and then a superb chocolate mousse makes its annual appearance. The recipe, which follows, serves eight.

MOTHERWELL CHOCOLATE MOUSSE

6 large eggs, separated
3 3-ounce bars of Lindt extra bitter-
    sweet chocolate with vanilla, or any
    good quality bittersweet chocolate

5 tablespoons cold water
2 teaspoons dark rum (optional)

Break chocolate into small pieces and put in a heavy iron or enamel pan. Add water and stir constantly with a wooden spoon over very low heat until the chocolate melts. Remove pan from heat and carefully stir egg yolks into chocolate with spoon. Chocolate mixture should be warm, not hot, or the eggs will curdle. Stir briskly until yolks are well mixed. Beat egg whites until very stiff. Carefully add egg-white mixture to the chocolate, taking care to fold the eggs into the chocolate with a spoon or whisk. Pour into a large glass bowl or into eight small dessert bowls. Refrigerate for six hours before serving. Serves 8.

Yours sincerely,

E. A. Carmean, Jr.

E. A. Carmean, Jr.

DOLPH BRISCOE, JR.

Dear Mr. Gardner:

I thank you for your letter of March 12th.

I am enclosing some recipes that I like very much.

Caramelized Bread Pudding

Butter
8 white bread slices
2 cups of brown sugar
6 eggs, lightly beaten
4 cups milk
2 teaspoons vanilla
1/2 teaspoon salt

Butter the bread and cut into cubes. In the top of a double
boiler, mix brown sugar with buttered bread cubes. Combine
eggs, milk, vanilla and salt and pour over the bread and sugar.
Do not stir. Cook over boiling water for 1 hour or until
custard is formed. The brown sugar in the bottom of the pan
forms the sauce. You can put the ingredients in a souffle
dish and proceed as above. I like to serve this with an entree
that has a sharp flavor, like maybe some mexican food. It
is good to keep in the icebox because it is a lovely light and
bland sort of dessert for people to eat before bedtime or just
a good wholesome snack.

With best wishes, I am,

Sincerely yours,

Dolph Briscoe

DB:jo

Enclosures

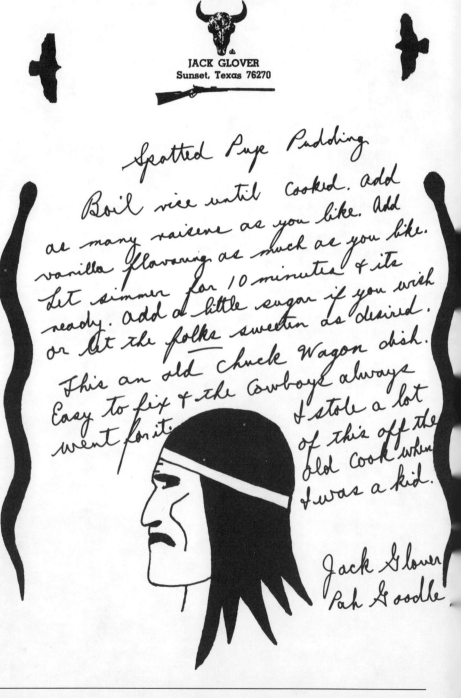

SUNSET TRADING POST
& OLD WEST MUSEUM

JACK GLOVER
Sunset, Texas 76270

Spotted Pup Pudding

Boil rice until cooked. Add as many raisens as you like. Add vanilla flavoring as much as you like. Let simmer for 10 minutes & its ready. Add a little sugar if you wish or let the folks sweeten as desired.

This an old Chuck Wagon dish. Easy to fix & the Cowboys always went for it.

I stole a lot of this off the old Cook when I was a kid.

Jack Glover
Pah Goodle.

State of Texas
House of Representatives
Austin, Texas

ROY ENGLISH
STATE REPRESENTATIVE
TARRANT COUNTY

Peanut Patties

3 cups sugar
1 cup Karo syrup (light)
1/2 cup water
3 cups raw unsalted peanuts
1 stick butter
1 teaspoon vanilla
4 drops red food color

Mix in heavy pan. Bring to a full rolling boil. Boil 5 minutes. Take off stove and add butter, vanilla and color. Beat by hand until thick and smooth.

Drop by spoon onto wax paper any size. Wait until firm. (about 1 hour)

Roy E. English

THE VICE PRESIDENT'S HOUSE
WASHINGTON, D.C. 20501

CHOCOLATE MOUSSE
(serves 8 to 10)

1 pound sweet chocolate
6 eggs
1 cup butter
whipping cream
vanilla or rum
pinch of salt
sugar
1/3 cup chopped nuts or grated chocolate

Melt the chocolate in a double boiler. Add the
egg yolks one at a time, beating each one in
thoroughly. Keep heat very low. Next add butter
which should be very soft, not melted. Beat
vigorously. Remove from heat. Beat the egg
whites stiff, but not dry, with a pinch of salt
and fold into the chocolate mixture thoroughly
so that no white spots show. Put in a greased
6 cup mold, bowl, or individual cups. Let
stand in refrigerator overnight. About an hour
before serving, turn out dessert. Dip into hot
water once or twice to facilitate turning it
out unto a plate. Frost with whipped cream
flavored with a little sugar and vanilla or rum.
Sprinkle with nuts or grated chocolate.
Chill before serving.

Barbara Bush

MRS. H. E. CHILES

Cherries Jubilee

Make ahead of time: seeded bing cherries (8 per serving)
put cherries in pan and cover with syrup from can. Add 2
teaspoons red currant jelly, 2 teaspoons of honey, cover
pan and bring to near boil. Before guests: add warm cherry
mixture to chafing dish and heat. Add Curacao, a little rum
and brandy, ignite and serve over vanilla ice cream or
cheese cake.
Tip: alcohol must be 100 proof to ignite at room temperature.
brandy (less than 100 proof) must be heated to ignite.

Banana Flambe
(two servings per banana)

Peel banana and slice (you may use waffle cutter). Sprinkle
with granulated sugar. In hot saute pan put 2 tablespoons of
butter and 2 tablespoons of honey. Add a few drops of lemon
juice and 2 ounces of orange juice. Add 1/2 ounce Grand
Marnier and heat. Place banana slices in pan; bring to a near
boil. Pour a bit of brandy and rum over them, ignite and
serve blazing over pound cake or coffee ice cream.
Tip: turn the lights down for the full effect! be careful!

These recipes are from my book PARTIES, PARTIES.

★ DESSERTS ★

STRAWBERRY-CREAM SQUARES

2 (3-ounce) packages strawberry gelatin
2 cups boiling water
2 (10-ounce) packages frozen
   strawberries

1 (13½-ounce) can crushed pineapple
2 large ripe bananas, finely diced
1 cup finely chopped pecans
1 large container sour cream

Dissolve gelatin in water. Add frozen strawberries; stir occasionally until thawed. Add pineapple and bananas. Stir in pecans. Pour half into an 8x8-inch pan and chill until firm. Spread evenly with sour cream. Pour remaining gelatin on top and chill until firm. Cut into 9 squares and top with teaspoon of sour cream.

Charles W. Evans
State Representative

ORANGE CUSTARD

2 oranges
2 tablespoons sugar
1 (13-ounce) can evaporated milk
2½ cups milk, divided

3 tablespoons flour
1 cup sugar
3 egg yolks
1 teaspoon vanilla

Peel, section and dice oranges. Sprinkle oranges with sugar and set aside. In a saucepan, combine evaporated milk and 1½ cups milk; bring to a simmer. Mix flour with sugar, add egg yolks and remaining 1 cup milk and stir until smooth. Add slowly to simmering milk, stirring constantly. Cook over low heat until mixture coats the back of a wooden spoon. Do not boil. Stir in diced oranges and vanilla. Pour into 10-inch ovenproof bowl or 8 individual custard cups. Spread meringue over custard, sealing well to edges. Bake at 450° until meringue is lightly browned. Serve hot or chilled. Serves 8.

MERINGUE
3 egg whites
3 tablespoons sugar

½ teaspoon vanilla

Beat egg whites until soft peaks form. Slowly add sugar and beat until stiff but not dry. Fold in vanilla.

Mrs. Darrell Royal (Edith)

QUICK PEACHES FLAMBÉ

This is a quick dessert dish, great for unexpected company.

1 can Elberta peach halves (8)
½ pound butter
½ teaspoon cinnamon

2 jiggers 100 proof bourbon
1 quart French Vanilla ice cream

Drain peaches and reserve ½ cup of syrup. Combine syrup and butter in a chafing dish or shallow Pyrex dish and warm over medium heat until butter is melted and thoroughly mixed with syrup. Add cinnamon and 8 peach halves, stirring and basting peach halves until heated throughout. Remove from heat and pour bourbon onto peaches. Divide ice cream into four dishes and bring to table. Flame the bourbon in the chafing dish until flames die, then spoon 2 peach halves and sauce on each dish of ice cream.

Joe Dickey
Southwest Conference Radio Network

RASPBERRY FASHION

4 eggs, separated
Pinch of cream of tartar
2 cups sugar
3 cups whole milk
1 packet gelatin
½ cup Chambourd liqueur

2 tablespoons cornstarch
1 teaspoon vanilla
1 (12-ounce) package frozen raspberries
2 cups whipping cream, whipped and
   sweetened
Whole fresh raspberries, to garnish

Preheat oven to 350°. Begin with egg whites at room temperature and add the cream of tartar. Mix slowly with electric mixer but gradually increase the speed until egg whites have soft peaks. Slowly add 1 cup sugar with mixer at high speed until meringue reaches frosting consistency. On greased cookie sheet trace 12 (4-inch) circles. Fill in circles with meringue. Place in oven then lower oven setting to the lowest temperature. Bake until dry. Boil milk. Soften gelatin in liqueur. Mix egg yolks with cornstarch. Stir in remaining sugar. Add mixture to hot milk. Place on low heat and bring to just a slight boil, stirring constantly. Remove from heat and pour into a bowl. Add vanilla and frozen raspberries. Place bowl in ice, chill until just set, then fold in half the sweetened whipped cream. Layer meringue with raspberry mixture. Frost with remaining whipped cream. Decorate with whole raspberries.

Rob T. Allen
Club Manager
Century II Club

CURRIED FRUIT

1 can apricot halves, halved
1 can pear slices, halved
1 can pineapple chunks
1 jar cherries

⅓ cup butter, melted
1 cup brown sugar
4 teaspoons curry powder

Drain fruit and pat dry. Mix butter, sugar and curry powder, and spoon sauce over fruit. Bake at 325° for 1 hour, stirring occasionally.

Diane Pate

CHERRY MOUSSE

1 can dark cherries with juice, seeded
1 cup liquid (cherry juice and water)
1 regular package cherry or raspberry gelatin

1 pint vanilla ice cream
½ pint whipped cream, whipped
Cherry Herring, to taste (optional)

To the juice from the can of cherries, add enough water to make 1 cup liquid. Heat to boiling and pour over gelatin. When gelatin has dissolved, stir in ice cream. Refrigerate until almost set. Add whipped cream and cherries. (If desired, add Cherry Herring, to taste but it's not needed.) Serves 10 to 12.

Betty Andujar
Former State Senator

MY HYPOCRITICAL MOUSSE
Gourmet dessert, but easy.

3 tablespoons Carnation hot cocoa mix
1 teaspoon instant coffee
2 cups milk
1 (3¾-ounce) package instant vanilla pudding mix

Dash salt
½ container Cool Whip (4 ounces)
Semisweet or sweet chocolate for curls, to garnish

Dissolve cocoa mix and coffee in milk. Prepare pudding according to package directions, using milk in which the cocoa mix and coffee have been dissolved, and adding a dash of salt. Let set for about 5 minutes, then fold in Cool Whip. Divide pudding between 4 or 5 sherbet glasses. Garnish with chocolate curls. (Curl chocolate by drawing a vegetable parer across a square or bar of chocolate which is at room temperature.)

Mrs. R. P. Klein (Mary Beth)
Wife, Mayor of Amarillo, Texas

CHOCOLATE ECLAIR

Graham crackers
2 packages French vanilla pudding

Cool Whip
Canned chocolate frosting

Line bottom of plastic coldcut keeper with whole graham crackers. Mix pudding according to package directions. Spread a layer of pudding over graham crackers. Add a layer of Cool Whip. Add another layer of graham crackers. Top with a layer of chocolate frosting. Chill until firm and cut into squares.

Harlan Streater

FUDGIE SCOTCH RING

1 (6-ounce) package Nestle's semisweet
chocolate
1 (6-ounce) package Nestle's
butterscotch morsels (1 cup)
1 can Eagle Brand sweetened condensed
milk

1 cup coarsely chopped walnuts
½ teaspoon vanilla
1 cup walnut halves
Maraschino cherries

Melt chocolate and butterscotch morsels with milk in top of a double boiler. Stir occasionally until morsels melt and mixture thickens. Remove from heat; stir in chopped nuts and vanilla. Blend well. Chill for about 1 hour until mixture thickens. Line bottom of a 9-inch pie pan with a 12-inch square of foil. Place ¾ cup nut halves in bottom of pan, forming a 2-inch wide flat ring. Spoon chocolate mixture in small mounds on top of nuts to form a ring. Decorate with remaining nut halves. Add maraschino cherries, if desired. Chill until firm enough to slice. Cut into ½-inch slices. Makes about 36 slices.

Mr. and Mrs. Jim Killingsworth (Margaret)
Head Basketball Coach
Texas Christian University

FOAMY SAUCE

3 egg yolks
¾ cup sugar
½ teaspoon vanilla

¼ teaspoon salt
½ cup whipping cream

Beat egg yolks, sugar, vanilla and salt until lemon colored. Fold in cream which has been whipped. Serve with fruit pudding or dumplings, and with apples. Note: The elegant chocolate soufflé is too frequently insulted with an innocuous sauce. All too often the rich brown crust is violated, and a thin, tepid vanilla concoction ladled into the soufflé's delicate heart. Soufflé and dessert lovers do not despair. Helen Corbitt offers salvation in the form of Foamy Sauce. Although not mentioned in the recipe, Foamy Sauce is an extraordinary complement to a chocolate soufflé! I have chosen to modify the instructions slightly. If a few teaspoons of unwhipped cream are added as the sugar and eggs are beaten together, the resulting mixture is much smoother because the cream helps dissolve the sugar.

William H. Koehler, Ph.D.
Vice Chancellor of Academic Affairs, Texas Christian University

COPYRIGHT 1957 BY HELEN CORBITT
REPRINTED BY PERMISSION OF HOUGHTON MIFFLIN COMPANY
FROM HELEN CORBITT'S COOKBOOK BY HELEN CORBITT

ICE CREAM

6 eggs
3¼ cups sugar
2 large cans Pet evaporated milk
1 pint half-and-half

1 pint whipping cream
2½ tablespoons vanilla
Milk

Beat eggs until creamy. Add sugar gradually. Mix with evaporated milk, half-and-half, whipping cream and vanilla. Pour into ice cream freezer and add enough milk to fill. Freeze. Yields 1½ gallons.

Mrs. F. A. Dry (Jan)

STRAWBERRY ICE CREAM

2 quarts strawberry soda pop
2 (14-ounce) cans Eagle Brand
   sweetened condensed milk

2 pints frozen or fresh strawberries

Mix strawberry soda pop with Eagle Brand milk. Slice strawberries into quarters and add to mixture. Pour into a 1-gallon electric ice cream freezer and turn it on.

S. A. Swanson, Jr.
Overseas Motors

THE BIG CHILL

Take 3 cups of sugar, then add 4
large eggs.
To start on your ice cream that
makes everybody beg.

Add 1 can of Eagle Brand plus a
can of Carnation milk large.
If you eat too much of this,
you'll soon resemble a barge!

Add 5 or 6 bananas and 1 tablespoon
of vanilla flavoring,
and I promise a mouthful of ice
cream worth savoring.

Put all in an electric ice cream
maker and fill to the rim with milk
and you'll soon have a fantasy
that tastes like silk.

Pack the freezer tight with lots of ice,
add the ice cream salt and wait
for your culinary delight.

Serve generous helpings a spoon at
a time
and your homemade ice cream will taste
　　better than fine wine!

Chuck Curtis
Head Football Coach
University of Texas at Arlington

FREEZER ICE CREAM

1 can evaporated milk
2 half pints whipping cream
2 pints light cream (half and half)

½ - ¾ cup sugar
Milk to fill freezer canister
　(about 1 quart +)
¼ cup vanilla

Serve with fresh strawberries, fresh peaches, or chocolate sauce.

Patty Harrington
Collections Registrar
Ft. Worth Museum of Science & History

LEMON VELVET ICE CREAM
Tastes like velvet.

1 quart plus 1⅓ cups whipping cream
1 quart plus 1⅓ cups milk
Juice of 8 lemons

4 cups sugar
2 teaspoons lemon extract
1 tablespoon grated lemon rind

Mix ingredients thoroughly. Freeze in ice cream freezer. Spoon into parfait glasses to serve. Ready to serve from freezer to table.

Mrs. Tom Vandergriff (Anna Waynette)
Wife, U. S. Congressman

DIVINITY

2 egg whites	½ cup water
3 cups sugar	1 teaspoon vanilla
½ cup white corn syrup	1 cup chopped walnuts

Beat egg whites at high speed of mixer until they are stiff and stay in peaks. Boil sugar, syrup and water mixture until it forms a soft ball when dropped in ice water. Pour half the syrup into egg whites, beating constantly. Cook remaining half of syrup until it forms a very hard ball when dropped in water. Beat syrup into the egg mixture. Add vanilla and nuts and beat until candy hardens enough to spread in pan lined with waxed paper or drop by spoonful on pan lined with waxed paper. Allow to cool.

Mr. and Mrs. John Ratliff (Robbie)

PRALINES

2 cups firmly packed brown sugar	2½ cups pecan pieces and halves
¼ cup water	1 tablespoon butter

Combine sugar and water and heat to a boil, stirring constantly. Stir in pecans and cook until mixture reaches the soft ball stage (235°). Remove from heat and stir in butter. Immediately drop by tablespoonfuls onto waxed paper. Let stand until firm. Yields 1½ dozen.

Mrs. Phil Gramm (Wendy)
Wife, U. S. Congressman

GEORGIA PEANUT BRITTLE

2 cups raw peanuts	½ cup water
1½ cups sugar	½ stick margarine
½ cup white Karo syrup	½ teaspoon soda

Combine all ingredients except soda and boil on high heat until light brown, stirring constantly. Remove from heat, add soda and stir well. Pour and spread thin onto greased cookie sheet. Cool.

Mrs. Lindon M. Williams (Evelyn)
Wife, State Senator

TEXAS
INDEPENDENCE
TRAIL

The San Jacinto Monument commemorates the battle which secured for Texas its independence from Mexico. As a result of the battle, Texas severed its legal ties with Mexico and embarked on a course which led first to a decade of independence as a republic, and ultimately to statehood, when Texas entered the Union as the 28th state on December 29, 1845. There are plans to renovate the monument for the 1986 Texas Sesquicentennial celebration.

(Photograph courtesy Texas Highways magazine.)

CITY OF HOUSTON

athryn J. Whitmire, Mayor

A FAVORITE OF MAYOR KATHY WHITMIRE

Mayor Whitmire is especially fond of Mexican food. The following is a recipe for HUEVOS CON CHORIZO.

Fry ½lb. chorizo mexicano (Mexican pork sausage) in frying pan. Add to pan six (6) eggs and scramble. Season with salt and pepper.

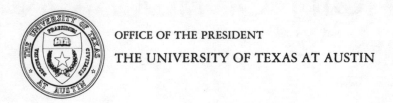

Dear Mr. Gardner:

I write in response to your letter of April 10 and I am attaching one of the Flawn's favorite recipes for jalapeño cheese pie.

With best regards, I am

Yours very truly,

Peter T. Flawn
President

PTF/hh

Attachment

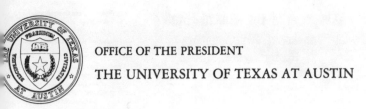

JALAPEÑO CHEESE PIE

4 canned jalapeño peppers

½ - 1 can chopped green chilies, drained

½ lb Cheddar cheese, grated

½ lb Monterrey Jack, grated

6 eggs, well beaten.

Cut jalapeños in half and rinse them under cool water, removing all seeds and membranes. Drain them well and chop finely.

Spread half of the grated cheese over the bottom of 7 x 11" pan. Sprinkle the chopped jalapeños and chilies over the cheese and top with the remaining cheese. Pour the beaten eggs over all.

Bake at 350° for 30-40 minutes or until the pie is set and slightly browned. Cool for 5-10 minutes and cut in bite-size squares.

Yield: 6 dozen

Congress of the United States
House of Representatives
Washington, D.C. 20515

COMMITTEES:

ARMED SERVICES

SUBCOMMITTEES:

PERSONNEL AND COMPENSATION
SEAPOWER AND STRATEGIC
AND CRITICAL MATERIALS
MERCHANT MARINE AND FISHERIES

SUBCOMMITTEES:

FISHERIES AND WILDLIFE CONSERVATION
AND THE ENVIRONMENT
PANAMA CANAL AND
THE OUTER CONTINENTAL SHELF
MERCHANT MARINE

SELECT COMMITTEE ON NARCOTICS ABUSE
AND CONTROL

Dear Mr. Gardner:

Thank you for contacting my office with an inquiry as to my favorite Mexican recipe.

I have found that one of the most integral parts of a Mexican dinner-- the tortilla--is one of the most difficult, unsatisfactory purchases to be made here in Washington. Therefore, I have come up with this old and simple recipe for flour tortillas. Fortunately the ingrediants are inexpensive because it takes a while to get used to handling the dough and capture the knack of rolling them out. However, once mastered, one can never go back to the tough store-bought kind.

With best personal regards and good wishes, I am

Sincerely,

Solomon P. Ortiz
Member of Congress

SPO/cg
Enclosure

Congress of the United States
House of Representatives
Washington, D.C. 20515

COMMITTEES:
ARMED SERVICES

SUBCOMMITTEES:
PERSONNEL AND COMPENSATION
SEAPOWER AND STRATEGIC
AND CRITICAL MATERIALS
MERCHANT MARINE AND FISHERIES

SUBCOMMITTEES:
FISHERIES AND WILDLIFE CONSERVATION
AND THE ENVIRONMENT
PANAMA CANAL AND
THE OUTER CONTINENTAL SHELF
MERCHANT MARINE

SELECT COMMITTEE ON NARCOTICS ABUSE
AND CONTROL

Flour Tortillas   (makes about 4)

2 Tbls. solid shortening or lard
1 cup All-purpose Flour
1/2 tsp. Salt
1/4 to 1/3 cup warm water

Cut shortening into flour and salt mixture until it is
about the size of rice granules. Mix in warm water
and work in with well-greased hands. Divide the dough
into shares slightly smaller than a golf ball and roll
out each on a floured board. Cook on a hot griddle until
both sides are browned.

Solomon P. Ortiz
Member of Congress

CITY OF LUBBOCK
LUBBOCK, TEXAS

ALAN HENRY
MAYOR

Dear Mr. Gardner:

Thank you for your letter concerning the recipes that you are compiling for a book. I appreciate the opportunity to supply to you some of my most favorite recipes. I look forward to receiving a copy of the finished product.

Mexican Quiche

1 Pet Rity Req. Pie Crust Shell
1 Can (4 oz.) Old El Paso Whole Chilies
6 slices bacon, cooked/drained
1 cup (4 oz.) Swiss Cheese, shredded
3 eggs
1 c. light cream
1/4 teaspoon salt
Dash Ground Nutmeg

Preheat oven and cookie sheet to 425 degrees F. Drain chilies and dry with toweling. Remove rib and seeds. Chop in large pieces. Crumble bacon and mix with chopped chilies . Sprinkle swiss cheese on bottom of pie shell, then chilies and bacon. Mix together eggs, milk, salt, nutmeg. Slowly pour over cheese mixture (the pie will be very full, but not spill over). Bake in preheated oven for 15 minutes. Reduce temp. to 350 degrees F and bake an additional 25 minutes or until knife inserted in the center comes out clean. Cool 10-15 minutes. Serves 6 to 8.

Mexican Chicken

1 cooked deboned chicken (chopped)
1 large jar of jalapeno cheese whiz
1 package Doritos
1 pound grated cheese
1 can Cream of Chicken soup
1 can chicken broth
1/2 cup chopped onions
1/4 cup chopped jalapeno peppers
1 teaspoon butter

Russell M. Gardner

Page 2

Heat soup and broth. Saute onions and peppers in butter. Layer
chicken, soups, doritos, onions, peppers and cheese. Top with jalapeno
cheese whiz. Heat at 350 degrees until it bubbles.

Best of luck to you and your worthy project.

Sincerely,

Alan Henry
Mayor

AH:os

KENT R. HANCE
19TH DISTRICT, TEXAS

Congress of the United States
House of Representatives
Washington, D.C. 20515

EL CHICO SOPAPILLAS

1-3/4 cups all-purpose flour
2 teaspoons baking powder
2 tablespoons shortening
1 teaspoon salt
3/4 cup cold water

Sift flour, baking powder and salt in mixing bowl.
Add shortening - cut in like you would for pie
crust. Add cold water gradually. Mix just enough
to hold together. Take out of mixing bowl and place
on a floured board; knead until very smooth.

Cover and let dough rest for 5 minutes. Then, on
a floured board, roll out to about 1/8 inch thickness
and cut into 3 inch squares. Drop Sopapillas into
deep fryer, 1 or 2 at a time, and when they surface
fan with the hot oil until dough begins to rise. Turn
the Sopapilla over.

When the Sopapillas are light golden brown, remove
from fire and drain.

Serve hot with honey.

LONE STAR BREWING CO.

Lone Star Fajitas

Soy sauce
Garlic powder
Onion salt
Coarse ground pepper
1 cup Italian salad dressing
1 cup Lone Star Beer
5 pounds fajitas (skirt steak)

Sprinkle meat generously with soy sauce. Cover on both
sides with layer of garlic powder, onion salt and pepper.
Knead spices into meat. Mix dressing and beer; cover
meat and marinate in mixture 2 hours or more. Put over
hot coals. Serve in fresh flour tortilla spread with thick
layer of mashed avocados. Add hot sauce (Pico de Gallo -
fine cut tomatoes, jalapeno peppers and onion.)

Serve with cold Lone Star Beer.

Patrick Dunavan
Buckhorn Hall of Horns

THE NATIONAL BEER OF TEXAS

*"Brewed from the world's choicest varieties of barley malt, cereal grains, hops
and Lone Stars' exclusive yeast culture."*

KIKA DE LA GARZA
15TH DISTRICT, TEXAS

Congress of the United States
House of Representatives
Washington, D.C. 20515

Dear Mr. Gardner:

As you requested in your recent letter to Mrs. de la Garza
I am attaching some of our favorite recipes for use in your book.

Kika's Texas Picadillo

2 pounds lean ground beef
2 large cloves garlic, mashed
2 large onions, diced
2 cups canned tomatoes, chopped
2 medium potatoes, cubed
1/2 teaspoon cumin
1/2 teaspoon pepper
1 tablespoon cilantro (same as fresh
        coriander or Chinese parsley)

Saute beef, garlic and onions in frying pan over medium heat
until meat is brown. Drain excess fat. Mix in all other
ingredients and cooked covered over medium low heat 20 - 25
minutes, stirring occasionally. This may be served with
refried beans, or as filling for tacos (corn tortillas) or
buritos (flour tortillas). Makes 4 servings.

With best wishes for its success and with kind regards, I am

Sincerely,

E (Kika) de la Garza, M C

mem
postage paid

226

POLICE DEPARTMENT

Dear Chris:

As you know, Mexican food is very popular in our area. We love Mexican food and regularly sample it at many of the area Mexican restaurants. An almost standard item at most Mexican restaurants is Salsa Picante or hot sauce. We found we liked most of the hot sauce served but always felt we could improve on it so we began to experiment at home. Through trial and error and probably hundreds of batches over the years we have developed the following combination of ingredients which suits our tastes perfectly. We love it and make it frequently. We use a food processor but you can also use a blender or chop the ingredients by hand. We hope others will share our enthusiasm for the Kennedy's version of Salsa Picante.

SALSA PICANTE DIP (Hot Sauce)

1 large can tomatoes
3 jalapeno peppers
1 small onion
1 small garlic pod
several sprigs of fresh cilantro
      or
1 teaspoon dried cilantro
juice of 1/4 large lime
salt and pepper to taste

chop the garlic until very fine. Add onion, jalapenos and cilantro and chop until pieces are approximately 1/4 inch or slightly smaller. Add tomatoes, lime juice, salt and pepper. Chop until ingredients are mixed and tomatoes are partially liquified but still a little lumpy. Refrigerate for about two hours to allow the flavors to mingle.

Salsa Picante is very good with fresh tortilla chips, spooned over scrambled eggs, or used as a low calorie dip with raw vegetables such as cauliflower, zuchinni, etc.

Thanks for asking for our recipe. We hope you and your friends will try it and enjoy it.

Bill Kennedy
Deputy Chief of Police
Technical Services Bureau

Earline Kennedy
Captain of Police
Internal Affairs

MEXICAN BUFFET

2 cans bean dip
3 ripe avocados
Salt, to taste
Pepper, to taste
2 tablespoons lemon juice
1 (8-ounce) carton sour cream
½ cup real mayonnaise

1 package Lawry's taco seasoning
1 bunch green onions, chopped
3 medium tomatoes, cubed
1 small can chopped ripe olives
¾ pound mild Cheddar cheese, grated
Ripe olives, to garnish

Spread bean dip in bottom of large platter. Mash avocados with salt, pepper and lemon juice; spread over bean dip. Mix sour cream with mayonnaise and taco seasoning; spread mixture over avocado. Sprinkle onions, tomatoes and olives over sour cream mixture. Top with grated cheese and garnish with ripe olives. Serve with round tortilla chips or large Fritos.

Mrs. A. M. Pate, Jr.

TEXAS PICANTE SAUCE

18 ceranto peppers or green chili
   peppers
2 garlic cloves

1 teaspoon Mazola oil
Dash salt
3 large cans whole tomatoes

Boil peppers in water until they have lost their bright color and are an olive drab green. Peel garlic. When the peppers are ready, put them in a blender with the garlic, oil and a sprinkling of salt. Grind until they are completely pureed. Turn blender off and add tomatoes. Blend them all together, pour into a large container. This makes about 1 quart and keeps well in the icebox. I also keep a large container of fried tortilla quarters which we call "tostados." They are wonderful to use with the hot sauce. This recipe has been in our family for years and is used with eggs and some salads as a dressing. There are a million things you can use it with. One seldom sees this recipe in cookbooks.

Mrs. Dolph Briscoe
Wife, Governor of Texas
1972-1978

TEX-MEX DIP

2 cans bean dip
3 ripe avocados, mashed
2 tablespoons lemon juice
½ teaspoon salt
½ teaspoon pepper
1 cup sour cream

½ cup mayonnaise
1 to 1½ packages taco seasoning
3 or 4 bunches green onions, chopped
6 medium tomatoes, chopped
2 small cans ripe pitted olives, chopped
1 package sharp Cheddar cheese, grated

Spread the bean dip in the bottom of a tray which has a 1 to 1½-inch lip. Mix avocados with lemon juice, salt and pepper, and spread mixture over bean dip. Mix sour cream, mayonnaise and taco seasoning, and spread over avocado mixture. Add a layer of green onions, then tomatoes and then olives. Sprinkle cheese on top and refrigerate until ready to serve. Serves about 20 to 25.

W. G. Blackmon (Genevieve)
Blackmon-Mooring

TEXAS EMERGENCY MARGARITA

6 ounces lime concentrate
6 ounces tequila
6 ounces Lone Star Longneck

3 teaspoons sugar
Ice

Pour all ingredients except ice into a 40-ounce (5-cup) blender. Fill with crushed ice (flake ice, for best results), blend and serve. Serve in salt-rimmed glass. Note: The combination of sugar and Lone Star is to compensate for triple sec. The reason for the substitution is to decrease the bitterness and add a more mellow flavor.

Tim Rogers
Mama's Pizza
San Marcos, Texas

JALAPEÑO CORN BREAD

2½ cups yellow cornmeal
1 cup flour
2 tablespoons sugar
1 tablespoon salt
4 teaspoons baking powder
3 eggs
1½ cups milk

½ cup oil
1 can cream style corn
8 jalapeño peppers, seeded and chopped
2 cups grated longhorn cheese
1 large onion, chopped

Mix all ingredients. Pour into 2 (11x9-inch) pans and bake at 425° for 25 to 30 minutes.

Mrs. Phil Gramm (Wendy)
Wife of U. S. Congressman

TORTILLA SOUP

6 fresh tomatoes, chopped
1 large onion, chopped
2 garlic cloves, chopped
1 fresh jalapeño pepper, chopped
2 (16-ounce) cans chicken broth

½ package Doritos
Sour cream, to garnish
Avocado, to garnish
Salt, to taste

Sauté tomatoes, onion, garlic and jalapeño. Stir in chicken broth. Crumble Doritos into separate bowls. Pour mixture over crumbled Doritos and garnish with 1 tablespoon sour cream and a couple of slices of avocado. Season with salt.

Mr. and Mrs. Coke Smith (Tracy)

MEXICAN MEATBALL SOUP

1 egg
½ cup chopped onion
¼ cup cornmeal
1 (4-ounce) can green chilies
1 garlic clove, minced
¾ teaspoon oregano
1 teaspoon salt
½ teaspoon pepper
1 pound ground beef
1 (16-ounce) can hominy

3 cups water
1 (16-ounce) can tomato sauce
1 (16-ounce) can tomatoes
1 tablespoon sugar
⅓ cup chopped onion
½ teaspoon chili powder
1½ teaspoons salt
¼ teaspoon pepper
¼ teaspoon oregano
1 (2-ounce) can green chilies

Mix first 9 ingredients and shape into 48 meatballs. Combine remaining ingredients, drop in meatballs and simmer for 30 minutes. Note: Try adding carrots, garbanzos or other vegetables of your choice.

Mrs. Darrell Royal (Edith)

GUACAMOLE SALAD

10 avocados, halved and seeded
1 cup diced tomatoes
1 cup diced onions

½ cup picante sauce
Juice of ½ lemon
Salt, to taste

Using a kitchen fork, blend avocados, but do not mash too fine. Keep some texture. Add remaining ingredients and mix well. Serves 12.

Gilbert Gamez
Tommy Gamez
Dos Hermanos Restaurant

FAJITAS AND PICA DE GALLO

8 pounds beef skirts (fajita meat)
Pepper
Garlic powder
5 (10-ounce) bottles Worcestershire sauce
1 bottle red or white wine
1 stick butter, melted
1 small squeeze-bottle lemon juice
1 medium can pickled jalapeño peppers
6 large ripe tomatoes

3 celery stalks
1 bunch fresh cilantro
1 bunch scallions
5 fresh serrano peppers
2 large onions
2 limes
2 large bell peppers
2 dozen flour tortillas

Have your butcher run the fajitas through the tenderizer at least once and also trim excess fat. To prepare marinade, use a large deep pan or bowl, add meat that has been peppered liberally and dusted with garlic powder. Cover with all the Worcestershire, half the wine, melted butter, lemon juice and 2 chopped jalapeños. Add more wine and water if meat is not covered. Let stand at room temperature for at least 3 hours. To prepare the Pica de Gallo, scald the tomatoes to remove skin by briefly submerging them in boiling water. After removing the skin, chop into cubes about ½-inch square or smaller. Place the chopped tomatoes in a 1-quart pitcher or bowl. Add finely chopped celery, 1 cup cilantro, 3 cups sliced scallions, serrano peppers, to taste. Stir and add more onions, peppers or cilantro, if necessary. Squeeze fresh lime juice over pica and refrigerate. Grill meat with sliced onions and bell peppers. Sear meat on both sides, then cook on reduced flame for 10 to 15 minutes. Baste with marinade if you like. Test meat periodically to keep from overcooking. Slice meat into strips about 1x3-inches. Place several strips of meat in a flour tortilla, add a spoonful of pica and guacamole and enjoy. Serve with refried beans and guacamole. Serves 6 to 8.

George M. Young, Jr.
Young Oil Company

TAMALES

1 (3-pound) can shortening (Crisco)
20 pounds masa (to make 30 dozen
  tamales)
½ cup salt, or to taste
3 cups meat broth
1 cup chili blend, or more for a darker
  blend
2 pork roasts

2 beef roasts
Pepper, to taste
¼ pound garlic powder
¼ pound comino, ground
1 pound chili blend
4 pounds corn shucks

Melt shortening and add to masa with salt, meat broth and chili blend. Mix well. Set aside. For 20 pounds of masa you will need 15 to 20 pounds of meat. I like to use 2 pork roasts and 2 beef roasts. Some people use all pork. Boil meat in a large pot. Add salt, black pepper, garlic and comino. When meat is tender and well-cooked all the way through, remove from stove and chop into fine pieces. Put back in pot and recook. Add salt and chili blend, to taste. Prepare your corn shucks. Wash in the kitchen sink about 3 or 4 warm water rinses. Leave soaking in water until ready to use. Separate leaves, rub your masa mix on the rough side. Add 1 tablespoon of meat mixture, fold ends toward each other and fold top under.

COOKING YOUR TAMALES

You will need a pot about 12x12 or taller. Lay some shuck leaves on bottom of pot. Use a small cup in the middle of the pot. Stack tamales at an angle all around cup all the way to the top. Pour in 3 cups of water and cover with a wet clean white towel. Cook until done.

Mr. and Mrs. Frank Chairez (Helen)

ENCHILADA CASSEROLE

2 pounds hamburger
1 small onion, chopped
1 package tortillas (broken in fourths)
1 can cream of chicken soup

1 can cream of mushroom soup
Mild enchilada sauce
1 large or 2 small cans green chilies
1 package longhorn cheese, grated

Brown meat and onion, drain and spread in baking pan. Arrange tortillas over meat and onion. Mix soups and spoon over tortillas. Spread the enchilada sauce over soup, sprinkle with green chilies and top with grated cheese. Cover and bake at 350° for 30 minutes, uncover and bake 15 minutes.

Mrs. Bill Sarpalius (Donna)
Wife of State Senator

MEXICAN CORN BREAD

1 pound lean ground hamburger
Salt, to taste
Pepper, to taste
1 extra large white onion, chopped
½ cup bacon drippings
1 cup stone ground yellow cornmeal
¾ teaspoon salt

½ teaspoon soda
1 cup milk
1 can cream style corn
2 eggs, beaten
1 or 2 fresh green jalapeño peppers
1 pound Colby cheese, grated

Season meat with salt and pepper, and brown with half the onion. Drain off grease. Preheat oven to 350°. Put bacon drippings in iron skillet to be getting hot. Mix cornmeal, ¾ teaspoon salt and the soda. Add milk and corn. Then add hot bacon drippings. Stir in beaten eggs. Put a little bacon drippings in skillet and sprinkle with cornmeal. Heat until brown and piping hot. Put half of cornmeal mixture in skillet. Add meat, sprinkle with peppers, cover with chopped onion and grated cheese. Add remaining half of mixture. Bake at 350° for 1 hour. Serves 8 generous helpings. Great with brown beans or black beans and a green salad.

Mr. and Mrs. Billy Joe Smith (Georgia)

PRONTO MEXICAN CASSEROLE

1 pound ground beef
½ medium onion, diced
1 (15-ounce) can Ranch Style Beans
1 (10-ounce) can Ro-Tel tomatoes
1 can mushroom soup

1 can chopped green chilies
1 teaspoon salt
¼ teaspoon black pepper
8 to 10 corn tortillas
1 pound Cheddar cheese

Brown ground meat with onion until lightly browned. Drain excess fat. Add beans, tomatoes, soup, chilies, salt and pepper. Simmer for 10 minutes, stirring occasionally. Spray an 8x8x2-inch baking dish with Pam, or lightly grease. Break soft corn tortillas in bite-sized pieces and line bottom of baking dish. Add part of meat mixture. Continue to alternately layer tortillas and meat. Top with grated cheese and bake at 350° for 30 minutes.

Mr. and Mrs. Gene O'Rourke (Wanda)

MEXICAN CASSEROLE
Simple.

Doritos
1 pound hamburger, cooked and drained
1 small can chopped green chilies

1 regular can "Husband-Pleasin" Ranch
  Style Beans
1 can cream of mushroom soup
Cheese, grated

Crunch Doritos over bottom of deep casserole dish. Sprinkle cooked hamburger meat over Doritos. Layer with green chilies, then beans, then mushroom soup. Bake at 350° for 20 minutes. Cover with cheese and bake another 5 minutes. Serve garnished with Doritos.

Karin McCay
News Anchor
KCBD-TV
Lubbock, Texas

FAVORITE SOUR CREAM ENCHILADAS

½ cup chopped onion
1 (4-ounce) can mushrooms
1 garlic clove, minced
2 tablespoons butter
1½ cups chopped chicken
1 (4-ounce) can green chilies, drained
   and chopped
1 cup sour cream

1½ teaspoons chili powder
1 teaspoon cumin
¼ teaspoon salt
¼ teaspoon pepper
Cooking oil
18 tortillas, thawed
4 cups grated Cheddar cheese
2 cups sour cream

Sauté onion, mushrooms and garlic in melted butter until tender. Add chicken, chilies, 1 cup sour cream, chili powder, cumin, salt and pepper. Pour oil into an 8-inch skillet, filling ½-inch deep. Fry tortillas until soft (about 3 seconds) and drain on paper towel. Spread heaping tablespoon of filling in center of each tortilla. Sprinkle with cheese and fold sides over filling. Place seam side down in greased 13x9-inch baking dish. Bake at 350° for 15 minutes. Spread with sour cream and sprinkle with Cheddar cheese. Bake 8 more minutes. Serves 4 to 6.

Dr. and Mrs. Ed Maddox, D.V.M.

JALAPEÑO DRESSING

CORN BREAD

2 cups yellow cornmeal
2 cups all-purpose flour, sifted
½ cup sugar
8 teaspoons baking powder

1 teaspoon salt
2 eggs
2 cups milk
½ cup shortening, softened

Preheat oven to 425°. Sift together cornmeal, flour, sugar, baking powder and salt into bowl. Add eggs, milk and shortening. Beat with rotary beater until smooth, about 1 minute. Pour into 2 (8-inch) square baking pans. Bake for 20 to 25 minutes.

DRESSING

1 bunch green onions
½ celery stalk, with leaves
¼ to ½ cup bacon drippings
1 cup water
8 cups corn bread, crumbled
4 cups day old bread
2 to 3 cups turkey broth or more (made
    from boiling giblets, neck, etc.)

Cold water, if necessary
1 cup jalapeño juice
Salt, to taste
Pepper, to taste
Jalapeños, chopped, to taste
Turkey

Chop onions and celery and sauté in bacon drippings. Add 1 cup water, cover and cook for about 7 minutes or until barely tender. Combine with crumbled corn bread, day old bread, turkey broth, cold water, jalapeño juice, salt, pepper and chopped jalapeños. (Add as much turkey broth as needed to achieve the right consistency.) Stuff turkey with the dressing and place excess in greased casserole and bake at 350° for 30 minutes.

Mary Kay Ash
Mary Kay Cosmetics

MEXICAN HOMINY

1 medium onion, chopped
Oil
1 pound ground beef
1 large can hominy
1 can tomato soup
1 can Ro-Tel tomatoes and green chilies

½ pound sharp cheese, grated
1 garlic clove
Salt, to taste
Pepper, to taste
Grated Parmesan cheese

Sauté onion in small amount of oil. Sauté meat and add hominy, tomato soup, Ro-Tel tomatoes, cheese, garlic, salt and pepper. Let stand overnight. Bake, covered, at 350° for 1 hour, uncover and bake 30 to 45 more minutes. Use Parmesan cheese on top. Serve with tossed salad and garlic bread.

Jack K. Williams
Jack Williams Chevrolet

JIM BROCK'S KING CRAB ENCHILADAS

BASIC ENCHILADA SAUCE
½ cup butter or margarine
½ cup flour
4 (10-ounce) cans red chili enchilada
   sauce (not hot)
3 cups chicken broth

¼ teaspoon oregano
¼ teaspoon cumin
2 teaspoons chicken stock base (Spice
   Islands)

First make enchilada sauce. Melt butter in a heavy skillet. Stir in flour and cook, stirring over very low heat, for 3 to 4 minutes. Do not allow flour to burn, though it is all right if it colors slightly. Remove pan from heat and let cool for a minute or so. Stir in enchilada sauce and chicken broth. Return pan to heat and bring sauce to a simmer while stirring with wire whisk. Add oregano, cumin and chicken stock base and simmer over very low heat for 10 minutes, stirring often. If sauce seems thin, continue simmering a few minutes longer. Cover and set aside.

FILLING
1 pound Alaska king crab meat
1 pound Monterey Jack cheese, coarsely
   grated
2 bunches scallions, sliced, including
   some of the green tops (1 bunch for
   filling and 1 bunch to garnish)

Vegetable oil
12 corn tortillas
1 (16-ounce) carton sour cream

Shred crab meat with your fingers, then combine with grated Monterey Jack cheese and half the scallions. Mix well to blend. Heat ¼ inch of oil in small skillet. Dip 1 tortilla at a time into the hot oil for a few seconds to soften, then dip in into enchilada sauce. Stack tortillas on plate as you finish dipping. Place some of the filling mixture in the center of each tortilla and roll it up securely. Place seam side down in an ovenproof baking dish, ¾-inch apart. Just before baking, reheat the remaining enchilada sauce and pour it evenly over top of enchiladas. Bake at 350° for 15 to 20 minutes. Before serving, top each enchilada with a large dab of sour cream and a sprinkling of remaining sliced scallions. Serves 12.

Jim Brock
Cotton Bowl Committee

MAMA'S PIZZA

Dear Russell,

I have contacted over 100 celebrities, and most of them say they don't know how to boil water (so we better include this recipe). Here are my grandmother's secret recipes:

Bar-B-Q Boiled Water:

Fill pan (any size) with water. Place charcoal briquettes in Bar-B-Q grill. Add fire starter. Light charcoal with long match. Wait till charcoal turns partially grey. Put grill over pit. Place pan of water on grill. Wait till water begins to bubble. Use choice of Dr. Pepper, Coors, or Vandervoort's milk to pass the time till done.

Campfire Boiled Water:

Start fire, place grill over flame (usually supported by rocks at side of fire). Place pot of water on grill. Wait till bubbles are observed. Remove carefully, handle is usually hot.

Gas Range Boiled Water:

Turn on gas. Place pot of water over flame. Remove when billions of bubbles begin to fight their way to the top. Set aside to cool.

Microwave Boiled Water:

Pour H_2O in styrofoam cup. Place in microwave; push 15 second button. Wait till you hear signal. Remove from oven.

Yours truly,

Chris Farkas

Chris Farkas

RUSSELL M. GARDNER is a lifelong resident of Fort Worth, Texas and is son of a prominent Fort Worth physician. Russell has attended the University of Oklahoma, Texas Christian University, as well as the Summer Academy in Architecture at the University of Texas at Austin. He is now attending school in Fort Worth majoring in Business Administration, and he is a member of Sigma Alpha Epsilon fraternity. Russell plans to graduate from Texas Christian University in 1987, then attend graduate school. He enjoys snow skiing, hunting, water sports, and is an avid weekend golfer. Russell was just 19 years old when he began this project 16 months ago.

F. CHRIS FARKAS is a lifelong resident of Fort Worth, Texas where his maternal great grandfather settled in the early 1870's. He graduated in 1971 from Texas Christian University with a B.A. degree in journalism. Chris also served as president of Sigma Alpha Epsilon fraternity. After graduation, he became a professional restauranteur as owner of Mama's Pizza restaurants in 1973. The chain has since expanded to 25 locations across Texas. Chris has served on the board of directors of the Fort Worth Chapter of Texas Restaurant Assn. and became president of the Tarrant County Chapter in 1981-82. He is also a member of Confrérie de la Chaine des Rôtisseurs, TCU Alumni Association, Century II Club, and the Fort Worth Club. Chris is an amateur archeologist, and an avid hunter, fisherman, and outdoorsman.

Index

★ T E X A S   C E L E B R I T Y ★

M

McCay, Karin, 192, 236
McClinton, Delbert, 64
McDavid, Dawn Queen, 123, 181
McIntosh, Willis C., 64
McMillan, John V., 97
McMullin, Dick, 101
Macaroni and Cheese, President Reagan's
Favorite, 74
Mack Wallace's Biscuits, 36
Maddox, Dr. and Mrs. Ed, D.V.M., 236
Maddox, Mr. and Mrs. Frank W. (Lucille),
110
Magic Cookie Bars, 192
Magness, B. Don, 178
MAIN DISH/GAME
Dinner for Two from the Wild, 127
Dove Breasts Stroganoff, 130
Dove Mangiamele, Mourning, 129
Dove Recipe, Texas, 129
Dove, Susan's Special, 129
Duck, Barbecued, 131
Laredo Chili, 130
Mallard, Souped Up, 131
Quail, Curried, 132
Turkey, Fried Wild, 132
Venison, Chicken Fried, Y. O. Ranch, 128
MAIN DISH/MEAT
Beef Burgundy, 92
Beef Stew, 81
Beef Stroganoff, 90
Beef Teriyaki, Stouffer's, 85
Brandywine Beef, 92
Breakfast Casserole, 101
Briskett, Boiled Beef, 77
Briskett, Dan Rather's Favorite, 79
Briskett, Three Day, 93
Chili, Billy Bob Barnett's World's Largest
Honky-Tonk Texas Style, 83
Chili, Laredo, 130
Chili, Patterson's, 88
Chili Recipe of Senator John Tower of
Texas, 96
Chili, Sheriff Lon Evan's Famous Jailhouse
Recipe, 80
Chili Squares, 70
Chili, Sue's, 96
Chili, Tex, 78
Chili, Tony & Jaclyn's London, 95
Egg and Sausage Casserole, 100
Enchilada Casserole, 234
Fajitas, Lone Star, 225
Fajitas and Pica de Gallo, 233
Filet of Beef G. F. Handel, 86, 87
Hearty Meal in a Skillet, 97
Lasagna I, 97
Lasagna II, 98
Meat Concern, 98
Meat Loaf, Aunt Helen's, 99
Mexican Casserole, 236
Mexican Casserole, Pronto, 235
Mexican Corn Bread, 235
More, 94
Pork Ribs, Apricot-Glazed, 101
Ribs, Bud with, 91

Rump, Roast *Republican*, 100
Sausage Enchiladas, 232
Spaghetti Sauce, Spacy, 94
Squash Filled with Meat and Rice, 99
Steak, Bar-Be-Que Southern, 91
Steak, Chicken Fried, 91
Steak with Mushroom Gravy, Seasoned, 93
Steak, Pepper, 75
Talagarini, 95
Tamales, 234
Travels with Charlie, 89
Veal Medallions with Shrimp and Lump
Crab Meat, 90
MAIN DISH/POULTRY
Baked Chicken Breasts, 111
Baked Chicken Breasts with Dried Beef,
111
Barbecue Chicken, World's Best, 108
Broccoli Chicken Casserole, 112
Burgundy Chicken I, 109
Burgundy Chicken II, 110
Calabaza con Pollo, Mary Grace's, 109
Chicken Breasts Gourmet, 103
Chicken Breasts in Sour Cream, 112
Chicken Divan, 105
Chicken Enchilada Casserole, 223
Chicken Marengo, Farrah Fawcett's, 107
Chicken Pineapple Pie, 113
Chicken Rosé, 111
Chicken Salad Pie, 113
Chicken Spaghetti, 106
Chicken Spaghetti, 114
Crunchy Chicken Bake, 114
Enchiladas, Favorite Sour Cream, 110
Heaven on a Bone, 110
King Ranch Casserole, 104
King Ranch Chicken, 115
Lasagne, Golden, 84
Walnut and Cheese Stuffed Chicken, 108
MAIN DISH/SEAFOOD
Crab Enchiladas, Jim Brock's King, 238
Crab Meat with Curry and Almonds,
Sautéed, 120
Crab in Shell, Baked, 117
Gumbo, Nancy's, 125
Herring Copenhagen, 119
Scallops Baked in Garlic Sauce, 124
Scampi Boca, 122
Shrimp, Creamed Coconut, 122
Chrimp Creole, 121
Shrimp Creole, Grandma's, 121
Shrimp, Dale's Divinity, 123
Shrimp de Jonghe, 120
Shrimp Remoulade, 123
Shrimp Royale, Papaya, 122
Shrimp Squash Casserole, 118
Trout, Red Snapper or Bass, Baked, 125
Tuna Italian, 124
Mallard, Souped Up, 131
Mama's Pizza, 239
Mama's Pizza College Station, 156
Mama's Pizza, San Marcos, 229
Mandel Brote, 192
Mangiamele, Mr. and Mrs. Paul (Lisa), 129
Manicotti "Maestro", 74
Mantzel, Tom, 198

246

A quantity of Limited Edition copies of the TEXAS CELEBRITY COOKBOOK signed and numbered by the authors are available on a first come, first served basis. A full-color 11x14 Limited Edition certificate suitable for framing displaying your name and book number will also be included. The book and certificate come packaged in a special gift box, and make a great collector's item of the Texas 1986 Sesquicentennial.

Please send me _____ limited edition copies
of the TEXAS CELEBRITY COOKBOOK
at $34.95 each.   _____

Texas residents add 5⅛%
sales tax ($1.87 per book)   Tax _____

Mailing and handling charges
$2.00 per book   _____

                              TOTAL _____

My check for _____ is enclosed.

Please bill my ___ MasterCard   ___ Visa

Signature _____

Acct. # _____

Exp. Date _____

Ship to: Name _____

        Address _____

        City _____

        State _____ Zip _____

Please provide the name(s) to appear on the certificate(s).

_____

_____

_____

Send to: **Gardner-Farkas Press, Inc., P.O. Box 33229**
          Fort Worth, TX 76162 817/870-2048

TEXAS CELEBRITY COOKBOOK
GARDNER-FARKAS PRESS, INC.
P.O. BOX 33229
FORT WORTH, TEXAS 76162

Please send me _____ copies of Texas Celebrity
   Cookbook.. @ $15.95 each _____
Texas residents add 5⅜% sales tax................ @   .86 each _____
Postage and handling................................ @ $2.00 each _____
Enclosed is my Check or Money Order in the amount of_____
Make checks payable to Gardner-Farkas Press, Inc.
Drivers license # _____ State _____
Please charge to my MasterCard or Visa No._____
Expiration date _____ Signature _____

NAME _____

ADDRESS _____

CITY _____ STATE _____ ZIP _____
                           (PLEASE PRINT)

TEXAS CELEBRITY COOKBOOK
GARDNER-FARKAS PRESS, INC.
P.O. BOX 33229
FORT WORTH, TEXAS 76162

Please send me _____ copies of Texas Celebrity
   Cookbook.. @ $15.95 each _____
Texas residents add 5⅜% sales tax................ @   .86 each _____
Postage and handling................................ @ $2.00 each _____
Enclosed is my Check or Money Order in the amount of_____
Make checks payable to Gardner-Farkas Press, Inc.
Drivers license # _____ State _____
Please charge to my MasterCard or Visa No._____
Expiration date _____ Signature _____

NAME _____

ADDRESS _____

CITY _____ STATE _____ ZIP _____
                           (PLEASE PRINT)

TEXAS CELEBRITY COOKBOOK
GARDNER-FARKAS PRESS, INC.
P.O. BOX 33229
FORT WORTH, TEXAS 76162

Please send me _____ copies of Texas Celebrity
   Cookbook.. @ $15.95 each _____
Texas residents add 5⅜% sales tax................ @   .86 each _____
Postage and handling................................ @ $2.00 each _____
Enclosed is my Check or Money Order in the amount of_____
Make checks payable to Gardner-Farkas Press, Inc.
Drivers license # _____ State _____
Please charge to my MasterCard or Visa No._____
Expiration date _____ Signature _____

NAME _____

ADDRESS _____

CITY _____ STATE _____ ZIP _____
                           (PLEASE PRINT)

TEXAS CELEBRITY COOKBOOK
GARDNER-FARKAS PRESS, INC.
P.O. BOX 33229
FORT WORTH, TEXAS 76162

Please send me _____ copies of Texas Celebrity
   Cookbook.. @ $15.95 each _____
Texas residents add 5⅞% sales tax .... @   .86 each _____
Postage and handling .... @ $2.00 each _____
Enclosed is my Check or Money Order in the amount of _____
Make checks payable to Gardner-Farkas Press, Inc.
Drivers license # _____ State _____
Please charge to my MasterCard or Visa No. _____
Expiration date _____ Signature _____

NAME _____

ADDRESS _____

CITY _____ STATE _____ ZIP _____
(PLEASE PRINT)

TEXAS CELEBRITY COOKBOOK
GARDNER-FARKAS PRESS, INC.
P.O. BOX 33229
FORT WORTH, TEXAS 76162

Please send me _____ copies of Texas Celebrity
   Cookbook.. @ $15.95 each _____
Texas residents add 5⅞% sales tax .... @   .86 each _____
Postage and handling .... @ $2.00 each _____
Enclosed is my Check or Money Order in the amount of _____
Make checks payable to Gardner-Farkas Press, Inc.
Drivers license # _____ State _____
Please charge to my MasterCard or Visa No. _____
Expiration date _____ Signature _____

NAME _____

ADDRESS _____

CITY _____ STATE _____ ZIP _____
(PLEASE PRINT)

TEXAS CELEBRITY COOKBOOK
GARDNER-FARKAS PRESS, INC.
P.O. BOX 33229
FORT WORTH, TEXAS 76162

Please send me _____ copies of Texas Celebrity
   Cookbook.. @ $15.95 each _____
Texas residents add 5⅞% sales tax .... @   .86 each _____
Postage and handling .... @ $2.00 each _____
Enclosed is my Check or Money Order in the amount of _____
Make checks payable to Gardner-Farkas Press, Inc.
Drivers license # _____ State _____
Please charge to my MasterCard or Visa No. _____
Expiration date _____ Signature _____

NAME _____

ADDRESS _____

CITY _____ STATE _____ ZIP _____
(PLEASE PRINT)

Reorder Additional Copies